REALIZATION AND ENLIGHTENMENT

REALIZATION AND ENLIGHTENMENT

By S. and M. Adam

First Printing 1996

Printed by:
Bay Port Press, 645-D Marsat Ct., Chula Vista, CA 91911-4649.

Publisher:
Adam Publishing, 5185 Fino Drive, San Diego, CA 92124.

ISBN 0-9649152-0-0

Library of Congress Catalog
Card Number: 96-96353

Library of Congress Catalog
Card Number: 96-96353

TABLE OF CONTENTS

INTRODUCTION

The substance of which the whole universe is built is the same substance of which our mind, thoughts, and imaginations are built. Two scientific approaches to knowing that substance are recognized.

The first one is atomic physics. It uses splitting of atoms and subatomic particles, and it explains the processes by mathematics. Using this approach we will be able to know the substance of the universe only indirectly with the help of instruments, and only in an unknown future, not now. Also, we will be able to create only concepts about it; we cannot see it or experience it directly. Moreover, this approach is accessible only to a few physicists.

The second scientific approach is to discover the substance of which our own thoughts, imaginations, and perceptions are built. By using this second method we can become aware of that substance directly - without outside instruments, not by concepts, and not in an unknown future, but in the present. The sages call this direct experience realization or enlightenment. It is accessible practically to everyone willing to undergo the necessary training of his own mind.

This book is a modern scientific interpretation of the old teachings of the sages. It outlines the way to insight into the nature of oneself and of the universe, i.e. the realization of the Ultimate Truth. The basis of the universe is consciousness that is impossible to define, but possible to realize by help of meditations. Such realization brings ultimate understanding and thus permanent happiness, contentment, and freedom from fear about one's own existence.

The book is divided into three major parts. The first part presents an explanation of realization from the viewpoint of the modern science, especially of the physiology of perception. The second describes meditations that can lead to realization. The third is a short outline of eastern philosophy, yoga, and some religions that presently have a relationship to realization.

This book was written in 1969 and published in Europe in 1991. The book aroused interest in the subject and helped some persons to realization. Therefore, we are presenting it with some additions to the American public.

We are very thankful to our teachers for their help on the path. We also thank everybody who helped correct and publish this book. Regarding the bibliography, we decided not to submit any list as it would be too long. There are almost no citations in the book. The subject of this book is eternal, the ideas are not new but very old. Just the interpretation is modern. We wish that the western way of interpretation will help interested persons understand realization and elightenment.

* * *

Motto:

Loving kindness and compassion to all beings in the whole universe.
Let well-being, happiness, and contentment prevail for all beings.
I pledge to help all beings to realize the ultimate Truth.
I am taking on the sins and pains of all beings, so that they attain realization of Truth without any effort.

Prayer of a Bodhisattva

SCIENTIFIC PERSPECTIVE

IGNORANCE

Ignorance regarding the basic philosophical questions causes suffering. When one recalls what he really is, one removes the ignorance about the basic questions:

What am I?

What is the universe?

What is the purpose of existence?

And so on. By knowing what one really is, one removes fear from his life and diminishes suffering.

The human mind is not a perfect tool for knowing the truth. Thinking is the most recent phylogenetic function of the brain and, therefore, thinking is still very inaccurate. It is based on memory. Memory, being an imagination of the past, is not the present reality. Therefore, thought cannot become aware of the reality, that exists here and now. Thinking can only create a concept about the reality. To realize a state of consciousness that directly and immediately sees the truth about oneself and the universe and thus removes all basic fears and doubts, a direct and immediate awareness and perception without interference by concepts is necessary.

TRUTH

Conformity of thought and fact is conventionally considered to be truth. We cannot consider truth as something that is subject to change.

Truth, as well as reality and fact, is not a consensus of opinions. For example, in the past, people agreed with the theory that the earth was flat, not round. Scientific theories also are not reality nor ultimate truth or facts. In the past, scientific theories were different from today's theories; today's theories may be outdated in the future.

That which can be influenced and changed through time and space or under different circumstances and conditions is not reality, nor is it the truth. Our personalities are so changeable and so transient that we are not the same person now as we were at two years of age, or what we will become twenty years from now. Personality is not the basic reality. Feeling of our ego ("I") can be delusive. Some mentally ill people think of themselves as being Christ, Washington, two or more people, or animal, or god, etc. There exists something that just imagines that it is ego (me); but, indeed, it is not ego. Not only existence of our personality, but, also, existence of the whole universe may be a long dream or hallucination, lasting our entire lifetime.

Where did we come from, and where will we go after we die? What really is this that is called "I" and what is a personality? Where is the feeling of "I" or of personality, after one dies and the brain falls apart?

Everything of which we become aware can seem to be real but has different degrees of reality. The least real are our thoughts, concepts, and imaginations. More real are our dreams, emotions, and feelings. Very real are our perceptions of body and objects. Yet all objects, including our body, are subjected to change and impermanence. No object or thought in the whole universe can be considered as the Ultimate Reality or Truth. Only that which is permanent, unchangeable, immobile, and what will not perish, even if the whole universe perishes, can be called basic reality. Something exists that is never submitted to change and cannot be influenced by conditions, space, or time and is beyond any doubt. Only that ultimate basis of everything can be called truth. Truth always was, is, and will be the same - simple, alone, unique, independent, not composed, unchanging and eternal. The purpose of this book is to outline a way to development of insight into that Ultimate Truth.

Truth should be based on facts. In order to find out what a fact is, let us analyze the way we perceive things.

What was I before my conception?

Was I the same as a child as I am now?

Is my personality the same?

What will I become? Where did I come from, where do I go? What is this that I call "I", or my person?

VISUAL PERCEPTION

Sight is the most important sense for cognition of objects. Therefore, we will analyze visual perception first.

Presently, we are aware of an object in the space in front of our eyes that has a white surface and is covered with black marks. We call this object a book. We see this book because light is falling on and is partially reflected by the book. We cannot see the book without light. In total darkness, we know the book is still there because we can feel it with our fingers even though we cannot see it. Thus, we know that we are not able to become visually conscious of the book itself because we need light to visually perceive the book.

The reflected light travels into the eye and falls on the retina of the eye. There, the light initiates chemical reactions in visual purple (rhodopsin - retin system). We cannot see without chemical reactions in the retina although we are not conscious of these reactions.

Chemical reactions in the retina irritate the endings of the optic nerve, and the optic nerve conducts this irritation to the brain. This conduction is, also, of chemical character; but we are not conscious of the chemical reactions.

So far, we know that we cannot become conscious of the book itself. We also cannot become conscious of the chemical reactions in the retina or in the optic nerve.

Right and left optic nerves cross over partially and continue as optic tracts. These tracts conduct chemical reactions mainly to the lateral geniculate bodies and from there to the calcarine fissures in the occipital lobes of the brain. There, the conduction causes chemical changes in the brain cells. These chemical changes can be spread to other brain cells by association pathways.

There, the physiology of perception ends. Physiology is not able to explain why we are not conscious of chemical changes in brain cells or why we are not conscious of mutually interacting

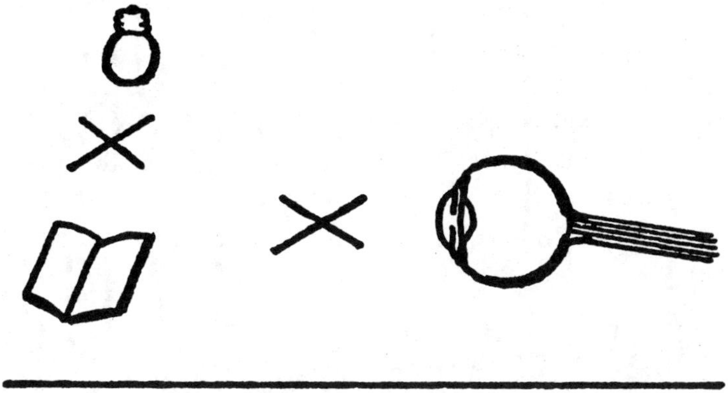

No light - no perception

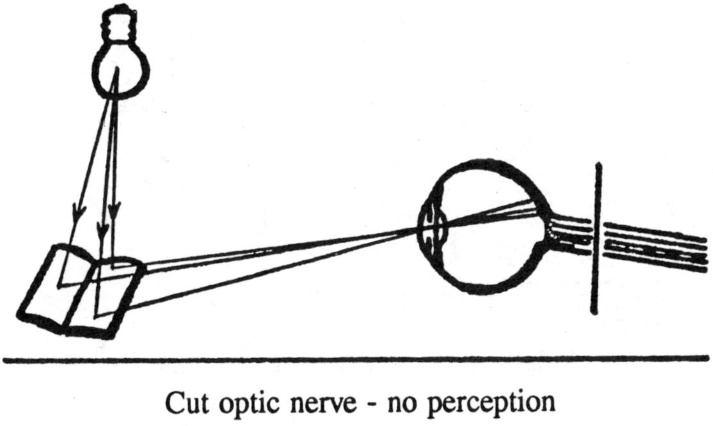

Cut optic nerve - no perception

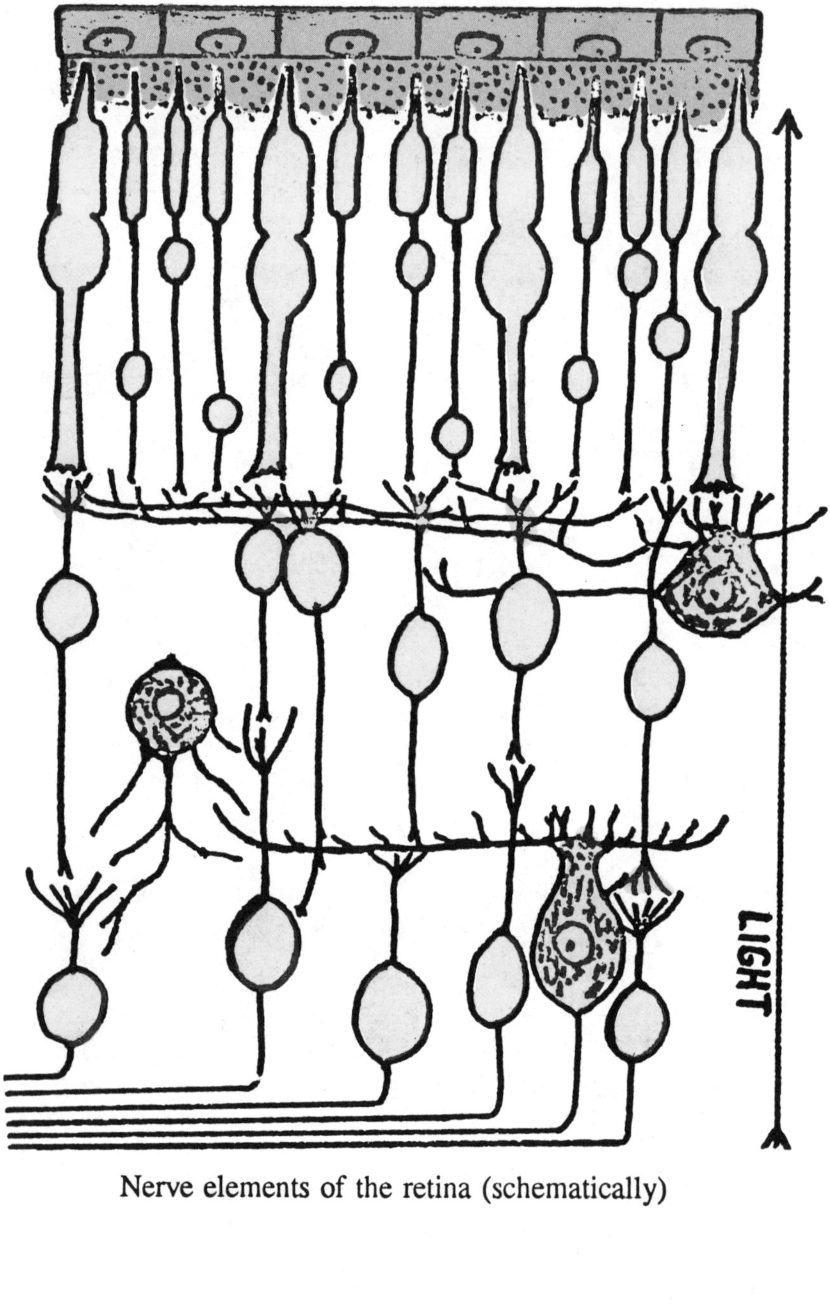

Nerve elements of the retina (schematically)

material particles like molecules, atoms, electrons, quarks, gluons, strings, or of whatever matter is composed. Likewise, it does not explain why we are not conscious of exchanges between energies like thermal, electric, magnetic, gravitational, and others. Physiology is, indeed, not able to explain the main point: why we are conscious of an image of a book that is white with black letters and that has a definite shape.

We cannot see the book itself; this means we cannot become conscious of the book that exists outside of our consciousness. We can become conscious only of the image of the book created by our consciousness. People who are unconscious, or people with hysterical blindness cannot see any object, in spite of the fact that their visual organs are intact. Hypnotized people, under the influence of suggestions, cannot see objects existing in front of their open eyes, or they can see objects that do not exist. Yet their visual organs and brains remain intact.

What is the difference between the world experienced while under the influence of suggestions and while in the regular waking state? Only this: we know that suggestions are experienced only by the hypnotized persons, and not by those who are not hypnotized. While under the influence of suggestions, those persons experience suggested imaginations as a reality and believe that suggested ideas are true. Only when the spell is removed, do those people realize that they were hypnotized.

Fallacies of perception also confirm the statement that we cannot become conscious of the object itself and that we are conscious only of our images about objects. For example: a straight rod submerged partially in water seems to be broken. In darkness, a rope is mistaken for a snake. Further, colorblind people cannot differentiate red from gray.

Hallucinations indicate that persons, under certain conditions, create within their consciousness entirely different imaginations about the world. They act according to these hallucinations.

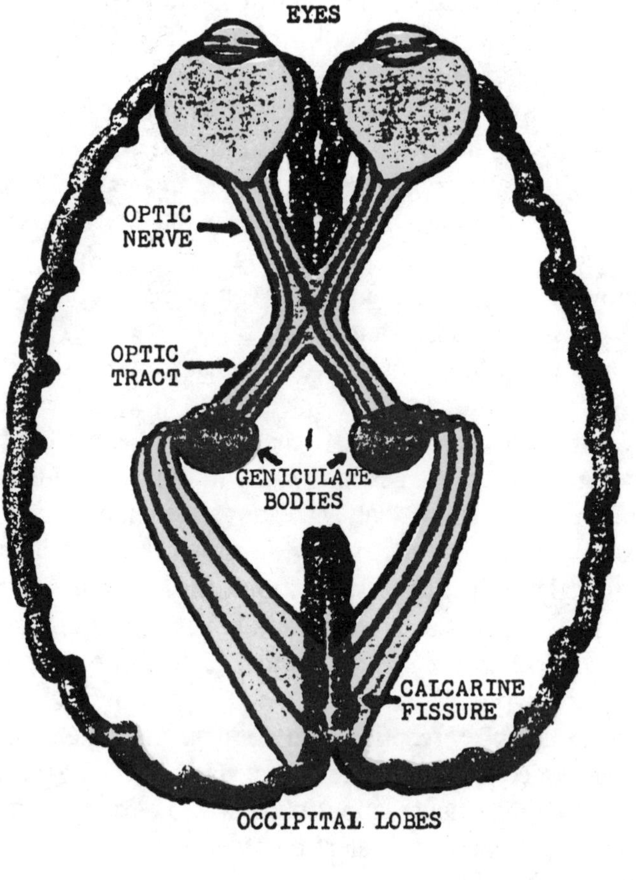

Schema of visual pathways

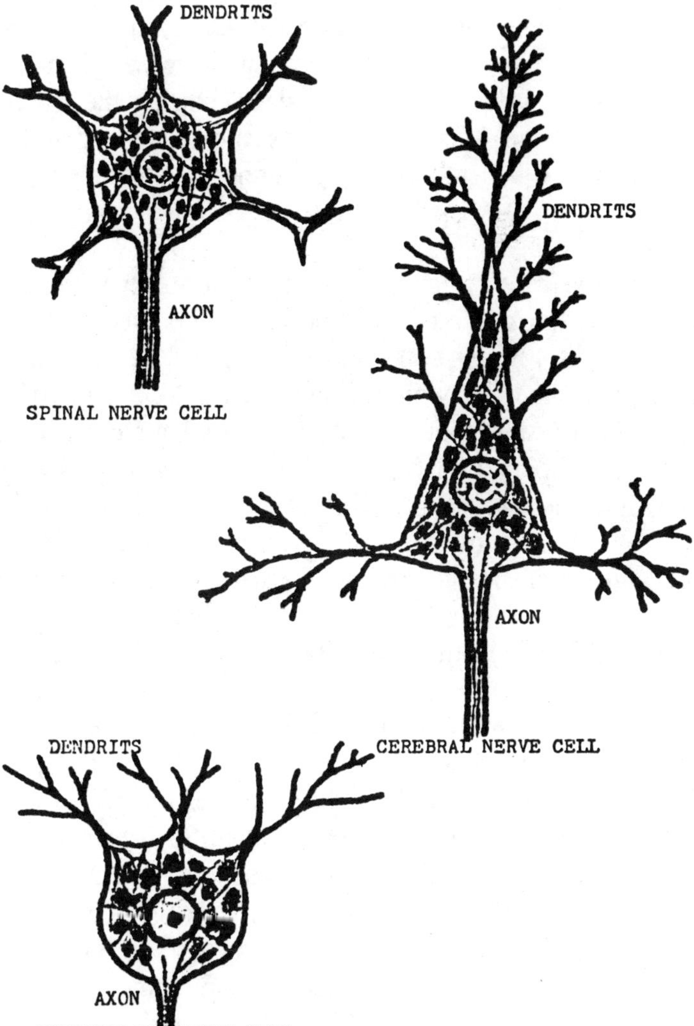
DENDRITS
AXON
SPINAL NERVE CELL
DENDRITS
AXON
CEREBRAL NERVE CELL
DENDRITS
AXON
CEREBELLAR NERVE CELL

Nerve cells

In our dreams we create a special individual universe for ourselves, and we usually believe in its reality as long as we dream. What is the difference between the world during a lively color dream and during a waking state? During the waking state, we know that the dream world was subjective and not seen by other people. When awake, we presume that other people, when they are awake, are experiencing images similar to those perceived by us.

In the case of seeing the book, we directly experience an image of the book in our consciousness. This direct experience of our imagination in our consciousness is a fact. We are not directly conscious of the book which is supposed to be outside of our consciousness. Existence of a book outside of our consciousness is, therefore, a theory (assumption, supposition). This theory is deduced from the facts existing inside our consciousness.

We are not conscious of the particles and energies of which objects are composed. In reality, we are conscious of imaginations of whole objects, which we interpret as things existing outside of us. Obviously we are unable to become directly conscious of objects outside of our consciousness, i.e. of things themselves, light itself, chemical reactions in the retina themselves, nerve conduction itself, or chemical reactions in brain cells themselves. Existence of all these objects and processes outside of consciousness are only theories deduced from scientific experiments and will remain theories - even if they were probable - because no one has ever seen atoms, electrons, positrons, neutrons, Z particles, W particles, quarks, gluons, strings, waves of energies like photons, or gravitons directly without a mediator (instrument). All that was, is, and will be possible to experience directly are imaginations of our consciousness in our consciousness. Thus, imaginations in the consciousness were, are, and will remain facts. Anything outside of consciousness is only a theory and never a fact.

We are conscious only of the forms of our consciousness. We know directly only the content of our consciousness. Anything

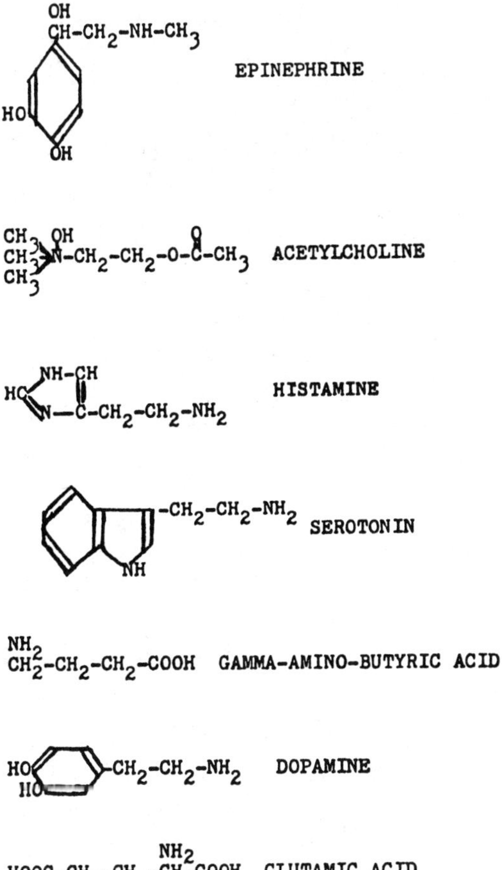

Some neurotransmitters

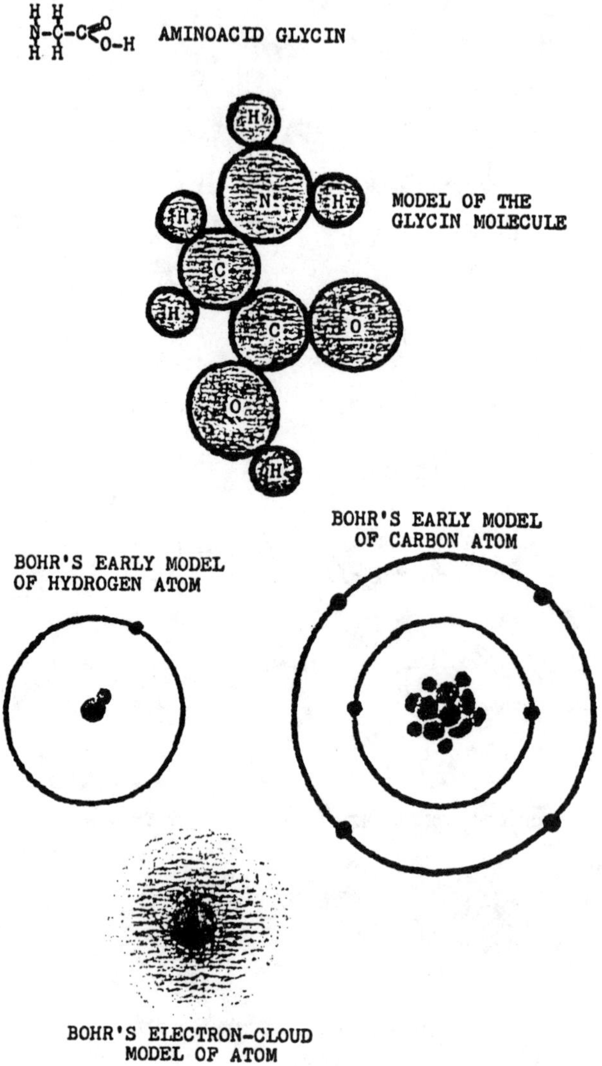
AMINOACID GLYCIN
MODEL OF THE GLYCIN MOLECULE
BOHR'S EARLY MODEL OF CARBON ATOM
BOHR'S EARLY MODEL OF HYDROGEN ATOM
BOHR'S ELECTRON-CLOUD MODEL OF ATOM

Models of atoms

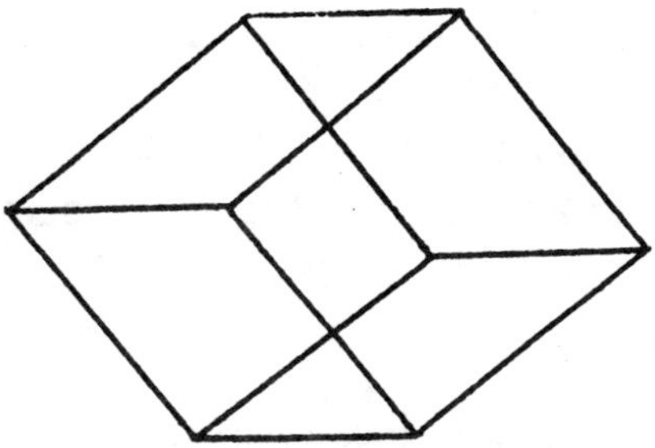

Necker's reversible cube

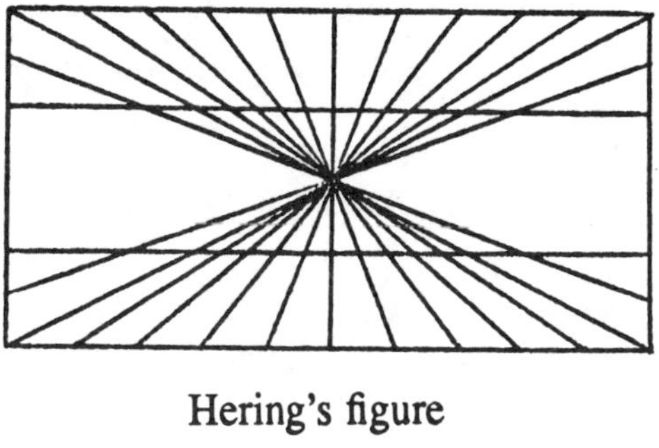

Hering's figure

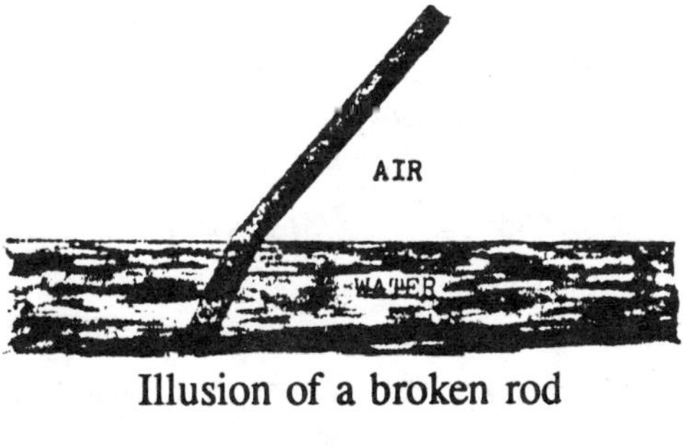

Illusion of a broken rod

else that we presume as existing outside of our consciousness, we must indirectly judge, conclude, and imagine by consciousness; and we create it of consciousness. All these imaginations are created from the substance of our consciousness. We cannot transcend our consciousness. Thus, the book we are seeing is only an imagination in our consciousness and of our consciousness.

By further observation and analysis, we find that there is no material book outside of consciousness and that two books: a material one outside of our head and another mental one inside the brain do not exist. Only the mental one exists. We find that the one who sees, the act of seeing, and that which is seen are not different but are the same. Such conclusions at first glance may seem to be incredible. Therefore, let us continue with the analysis of other perceptions: hearing, smelling, tasting, touching, and other senses.

AUDITORY PERCEPTION

Vibration of objects causes vibration of air. We cannot hear without vibrations of air, gas, fluid, or firm medium. On the moon, there is no air; therefore, speech must be transmitted by radio waves. We are not directly conscious of these vibrations of objects, air, or radio waves during the process of hearing.

Vibration of air causes vibration of the eardrum. Vibration of the eardrum causes vibration of the middle ear ossicles (hammer, anvil and stirrup). We are not conscious of vibrations of the eardrum or of the middle ear ossicles. Since middle ear ossicles intensify the vibrations about 20 times, we cannot hear the intensity of eardrum vibrations.

The intensified vibrations are then transmitted into cochlear fluid, which is in the inner ear. There are little membranes with hair, sensitive to vibration, positioned in the fluid. Again, we are

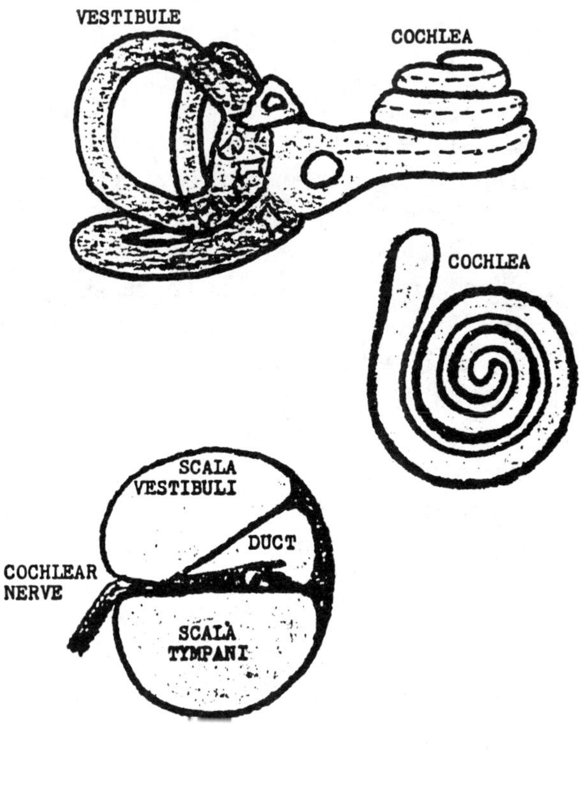

Schema of the inner ear

not conscious of vibrations of the fluid, membranes, and hair in the cochlea.

Vibrations of cochlear membranes and hair irritate the endings of the auditory nerve. Here, the quality of mechanical vibrations is transformed into the quality of chemical reactions in the nerve. Again, we are not conscious of that transformation or of chemical changes in the auditory nerve. Chemical changes in the auditory nerve are further conducted through the cochlear nuclei in the brain stem mostly to the medial geniculate bodies and from there to superior temporal gyri of the brain. Eventually, they may be conducted by association pathways to other brain areas.

According to physiology, the process of auditory perception ends in brain cells as chemical reactions. We are not conscious of the chemical reactions in the nerve cells of the brain. We are conscious of sounds which are of low or high pitch and of certain degrees of intensity. How these chemical reactions change into sounds, scientists are not able to explain. During auditory perceptions, we are not conscious of outside vibrations; we are solely conscious of our imaginations of sounds constructed by our consciousness only in partial accordance with sensory stimuli. For example, we cannot become conscious of certain very high pitched sounds that can be perceived by dogs.

Objective sounds (sounds themselves), supposedly located outside of our consciousness, are something of which we will never be able to become directly conscious. We can only assume that such objective sounds exist outside of us, but we will never be able to prove beyond any doubt that they really do exist outside of consciousness.

We have the firsthand proof that our imagination of sounds exists in our consciousness because we directly and immediately experience sounds in our consciousness. Facts (realities) existing in our consciousness are facts beyond any doubt. Sounds outside of our consciousness are only suppositions, presumptions, or theories and will forever remain so. These may be the most practical

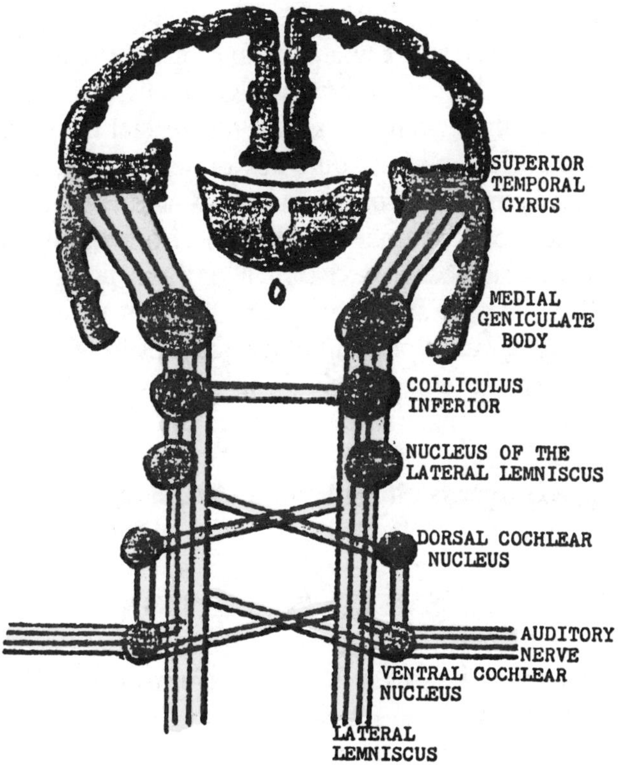

Schema of auditory pathways

theories but, when precisely analyzed, they are not facts. A fact is only that of which we are directly and immediately conscious.

Auditory hallucinations experienced by mentally ill patients are facts existing in their consciousness even though there are no vibrations of outside objects or of their eardrums; nor is there irritation of their auditory nerves to cause these facts to be experienced by their consciousness. Diseases of the cochlea, auditory nerve, or areas of brain related to auditory perceptions can, also, cause hallucinations of sounds without outside vibrations.

We can attempt to interpret sounds by physical and chemical theories, but we cannot explain the special qualities of sounds by these theories. Various qualities of sound, color, taste, smell, touch, space, time, etc. in our consciousness are entirely different from homogenous material particles and from any known forms of energy which supposedly exist outside of our consciousness.

Factually we are directly conscious of color, sound, taste, smell, touch, space, time, and other qualities in our consciousness. However, we are not conscious of objects outside of our consciousness, of the material particles of objects, nor of the chemical reactions in our brain cells.

To perceive anything is to imagine it by our consciousness.

SMELL PERCEPTION

Vapors and gases touch the endings of the olfactory nerve in the nose and react chemically with them, but we are not conscious of the gases or of these chemical reactions. Nerve irritation by these gasses in the nose is conducted by nerve filaments through the olfactory tract mainly to the parts of the brain called amygdaloid nuclei, paraolfactory areas, and subcallosal gyri. The conduction provokes chemical changes in brain cells in these areas and, by association pathways, in some other areas of the brain as well. Here the physiological explanation of olfactory perception

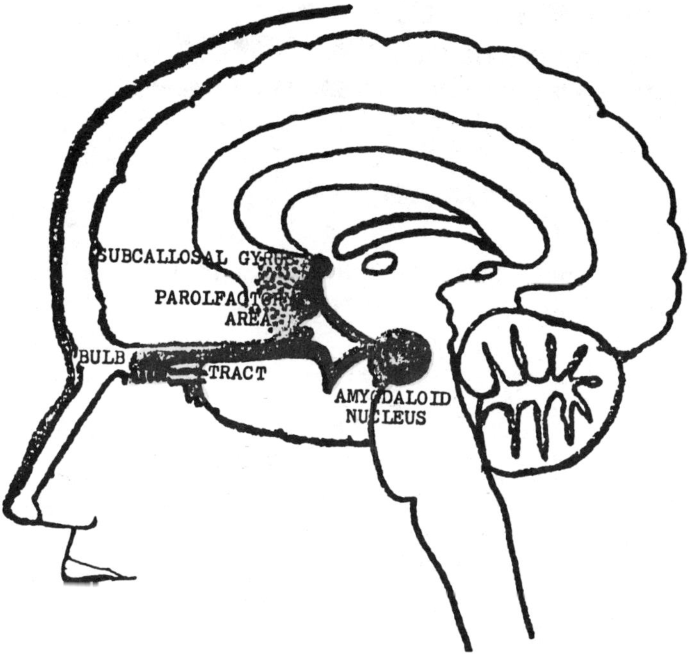

Schema of main olfactory pathways

ends. But, we know that we are not conscious of the olfactory tract, the amygdaloid nuclei, or the parolfactory area; and we know that the quality of smell is not identical with chemical reactions in these areas.

In all nerve cells, chemical reactions are assumed to be uniform and identical in all kinds of sensory perceptions and imaginations; but, imaginations of color, sound, odor, touch, space, time, and others are very different from each other. They cannot be identified with uniform chemical reactions of the qualitatively same material particles in the brain cells.

It is difficult for us to admit that we can become aware only of our imaginations when most of us have firmly believed that we have been directly aware of material things outside of us.

TASTE PERCEPTION

Taste endings in the mouth react with the chemical composition of the material coming in contact with the taste buds. Chemical reactions in the taste buds cause chemical irritations in the nerve endings of branches of the facial and glossopharyngeal nerves. As with other sensory perceptions, we are not aware of the tasted material itself or of the nerve irritations.

Nerve impulses are then transmitted through these nerves by chemical-electrical means into the brain stem and relayed through solitary nucleus and thalamus to the fissure of Sylvius in the cerebral cortex. Nerve impulses end there as chemical reactions in the brain cells. Thus says physiology.

Sweet, bitter, sour, and salt qualities of taste are quite different from the qualities of basic material particles known, so far, by chemistry and physics. The theory comparing the atom to a solar system is apparently not correct or definite. We do not know of any form of energy that is sweet, bitter, sour, salty, white, black, red, green, blue, yellow, high pitched, low pitched,

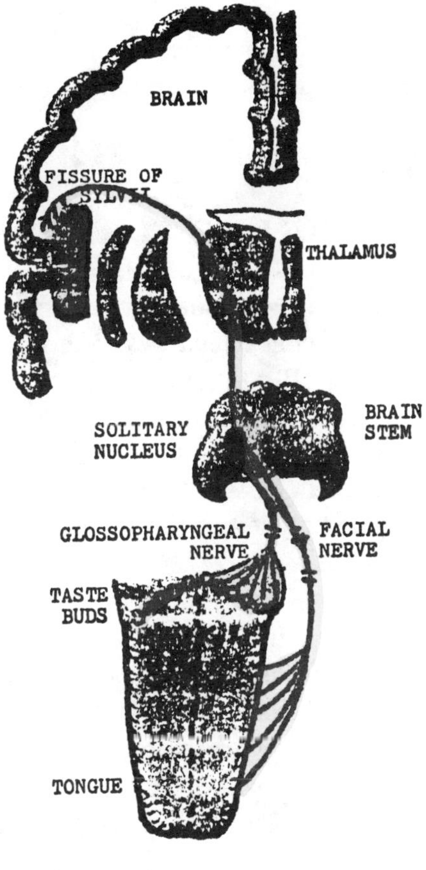

Schema of taste pathways

pleasant or unpleasant smelling, etc. by which we could explain imaginations of taste, color, sound, smell, etc. in our consciousness.

In spite of the incapability of physiology to explain perceptions by contemporary theories, it remains a fact that these imaginations exist in our consciousness; otherwise, we would not be able to be conscious of them. Consciousness creates these imaginations from itself and within itself and then wrongly assumes that it's imaginations exist somewhere outside of it as an independent reality.

TACTILE PERCEPTIONS

Free nerve endings in bodily tissues react to crude touch, heavy pressure, and chemical changes. Meissner's corpuscles in the skin respond specifically to light touch.

We are not conscious of the chemical reactions in the corpuscles or the nerve endings. From these nerve endings chemical reactions are transmitted mostly through the spine to groups of cells in the brain called nuclei (nucleus cuneatus, nucleus gracilis, thalamus, hypothalamus). The transmission ends mostly in the somesthetic part of the brain cortex located in the parietal area as chemical reactions in the brain cells.

We are not conscious of these chemical reactions in the brain cells. We are conscious only of the imagination of touch, hardness, firmness, plasticity, softness, etc. in our consciousness. These feelings are an imagination created by our consciousness.

It is especially important to be aware that any hard and firm feeling between our fingers, for example, when we hold a book or squeeze a stone is only an imagination in our consciousness and does not exist in the book nor in the stone themselves. These concrete feelings of reality are created by our consciousness of the substance of our consciousness and do not exist outside of it.

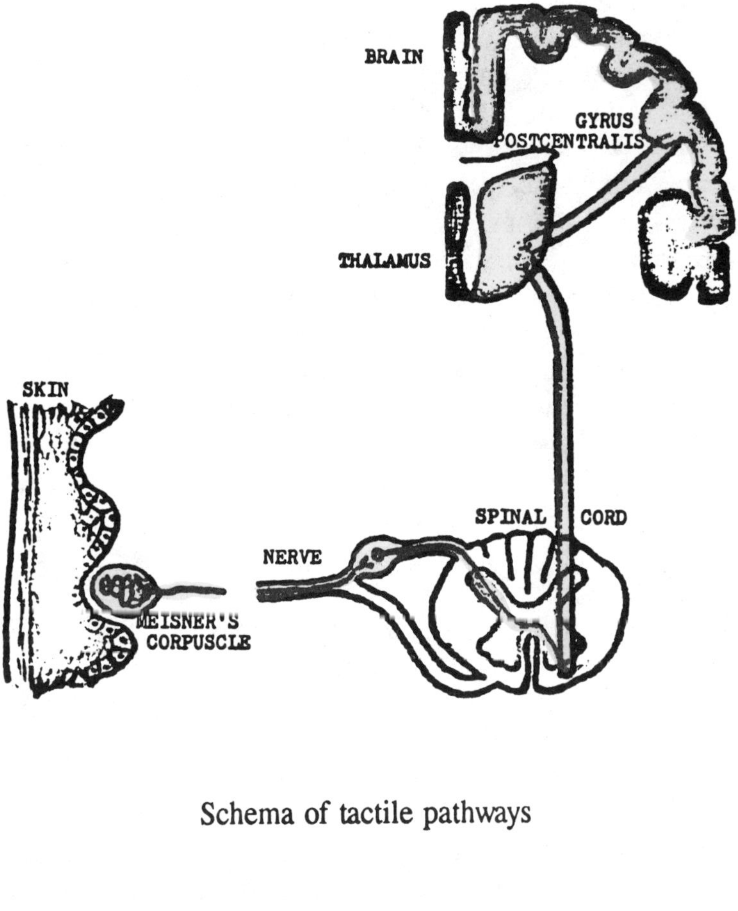

Schema of tactile pathways

Failure to accept this fact keeps alive our delusions about hard, firm, unchanging matter supposedly existing outside of our consciousness.

Physics state that matter is something changeable and is in constant movement. It consists more of empty space than of material particles. Exact analysis of perceptions shows that feelings of firm and stable matter are exclusively an imagination created by our consciousness. Even a large rocky mountain and, indeed, the whole earth and the universe are in an unceasing state of change and motion. We delude ourselves about unchanging, heavy, firm, and stable material because we do not perceive subtle motions and changes in it; and we do not live long enough to see the decomposition or destruction of this material.

It is important to always be aware that hardness, firmness, heaviness, immobility, reality, and unchangeability all exist exclusively in our consciousness and not outside of it. Outside of our consciousness, nothing is real, firm, immobile, stable, or unchanging. These delusions about firm, unchangeable objects are figments of our consciousness about the outside world. Consciousness itself creates these feelings of hardness, firmness, immobility, reality, stability, heaviness, and unchangeability. Consciousness creates them of itself, of the substance of consciousness. Consciousness itself - and not anything outside of consciousness - is real, hard, firm, immobile, stable, and unchanging. We just mistakenly project the reality and stability of our consciousness onto these objects.

The fact of existence of consciousness is the most basic fact.

STEREOGNOSTIC PERCEPTION

Position and movement of the head cause pressure on the vestibular nerve endings in three semicircular canals of the inner

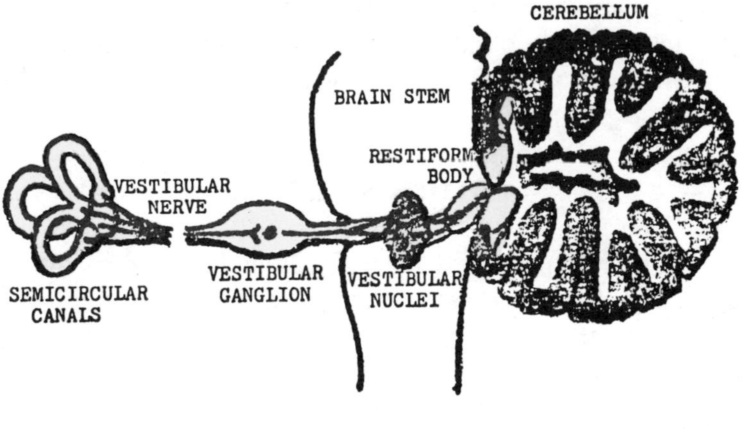

Schema of vestibular pathways

ear. This pressure causes chemical reactions in the vestibular nerve that conducts these chemical reactions to the vestibular nuclei and the restiform body in the brain stem. From there, the nerve conduction goes mostly to the flocullonodular lobe in the cerebellum.

We feel the position of our head in space. This feeling in our consciousness is, again, a totally different quality from chemical reactions. It cannot be identified with interactions of material particles in the flocullonodular lobe of cerebellum because particles are supposed to be built of the same material quality for all the senses.

This conclusion is the same as conclusions regarding other senses: the feeling of the position of the head in space is an imagination created by consciousness. We create our own space and our own subjective world in our consciousness that cannot be experienced by anybody else. Thus, every being lives in it's own subjective universe, created by it's own consciousness.

OTHER SENSES

Warmth is perceived by Ruffini's end organs in the skin and is transmitted by nerves to the spinal cord, then through the spinal cord to the brain. We are directly conscious only of the feeling of warmth, which is an imagination of our consciousness. This means that the feeling of warmth is a product of our consciousness and not something existing outside of our consciousness. The vibration frequency of molecules of objects is qualitatively different from warm and cold feelings.

In the case of cold perception, the process is similar to the perception of warmth. Krause's end bulbs in the skin respond specifically to cold objects.

The transmitting velocity in the nerve fibers differs remarkably among different types of nerve fibers. In type A fibers, the velocity is as high as 100 meters per second; in type C fibers,

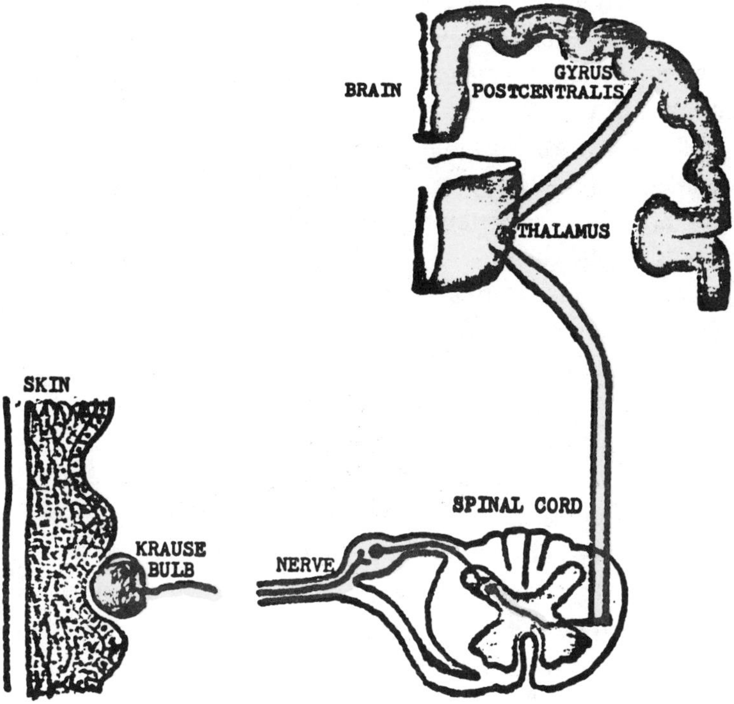

Schema of cold perception pathways

it is as low as 1 meter per second. Therefore, some perceptions are faster than others; and we are conscious, for example, of pain later than of cold or hot. This time difference, again, proves that we are not aware of objects outside of our consciousness, but are only of imaginations about the objects within our consciousness. We touch an object at the same time, but we become conscious of touch and of pain at different times.

We have many more senses than five. For example, Golgi's tendon apparatus reacts to the degree of tension in tendons. Muscle spindles react to the degree of stretch of muscle fibers. Pacinian corpuscles detect vibrations (rapid changes in pressure). Stretch receptors in walls of arteries react to the blood pressure in arteries. There are similar stretch receptors for pressure in veins, lungs, and other visceral organs. Chemical receptors in the brain, especially in hypothalamus and in special bodies at the aorta and at carotid arteries called aortic and carotid bodies, react to chemical changes in the blood.

Many of these senses usually do not provoke specific feelings, nor do they influence consciousness; but when they increase in intensity, they may cause feelings of tension, pressure, fullness, choking, anxiety, or other indefinite feelings. To stress again, all these qualities of perceptions like tension, choking, anxiety, pressure, fullness, etc., do not exist at the site of mechanical or chemical stimulations. They exist exclusively as imaginations in the consciousness.

There are a variety of other specialized receptors, not described here, reacting to specific types of stimuli. All receptors can be analyzed in a manner similar to sight, hearing, smell, touch and other senses.

The whole world, that we are aware of, is only our consciousness. The whole universe is only an imagination in consciousness.

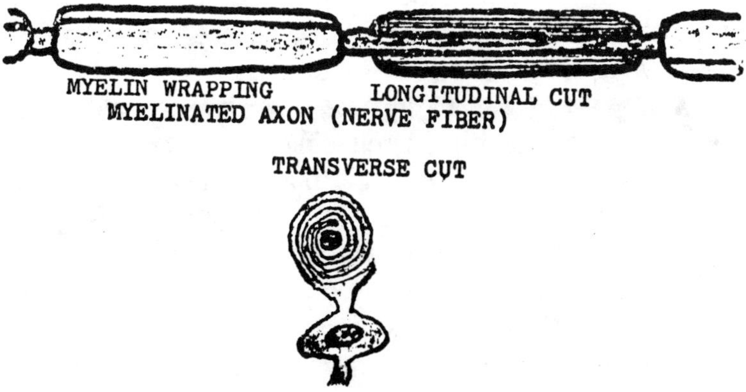

Myelinated axon (nerve fiber)

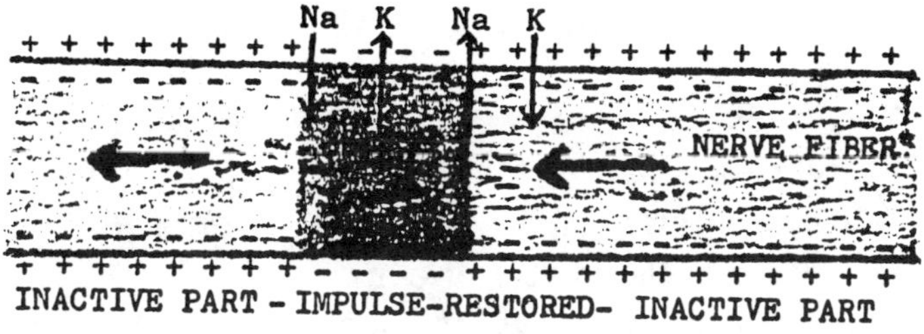

Exchange of Natrium and Kalium ions during a nerve impulse

PERCEPTION OF THE BODY

So far by studying the physiology of perception, we have understood that all things and all the universe which we perceive and of which we are conscious are only an imagination created by our consciousness. The next step to be understood is the perception of our body. We are conscious of our body in the same way as we are of everything else; in order to be conscious of our body, the body must be in our consciousness. We cannot become conscious of a body which is outside of consciousness.

We are conscious of our body and its surroundings. This means that the body and its surroundings are in the consciousness and that our consciousness is larger than the body. The same, of course, applies to our head and brain. We are conscious of our head; therefore, our consciousness is not in the head or in the brain, but the head and brain are in our consciousness. Consciousness is larger than the head and body. The skin limits our body, but the skin does not limit our consciousness. Consciousness has no firm borders.

Consciousness is the common denominator that unifies the body and its environment. Consciousness underlies the whole perceived universe including our body.

FEELING OF THE EGO

The feeling of our ego ("I") is not dependent on the feeling of our body. We usually feel our ego in the middle of our chest or head. When we point at ourselves, saying "I" or "me" we do it by pointing a finger to the middle of our chest.

In our imagination, we can remove any part of our body without removing or reducing our feeling of ego. We can cut off our hands and our ego feeling will not be diminished. We can cut off both legs and the ego feeling will not be changed. We can even

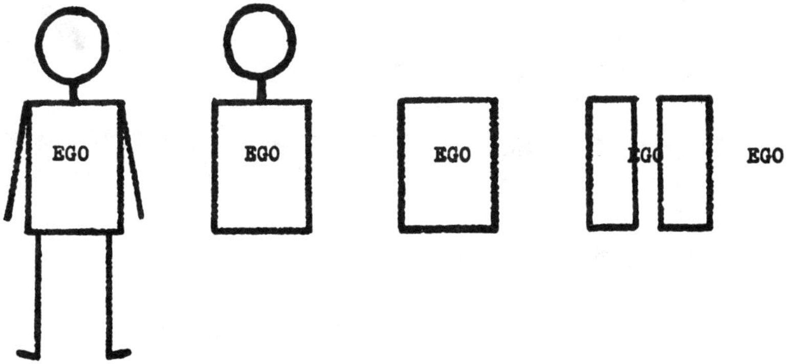

We are able to separate the feeling of ego ("I") from the feeling of the body and personality. Ego is a thought (idea).

mentally split our abdomen and our chest or head into two equal parts, and still we can feel our ego with the same or greater intensity. We can separate our ego feeling from body feeling.

When we observe our thinking, we discover that the thought of oneself comes before the feeling of oneself and the feeling of personality. Physical pain comes first; then pain arouses the thought of oneself; and after the feeling of oneself, the feeling of personality, that is of the "me," arises. If we are able to look at the body impersonally, not identifying ourselves with it as though the body were just another object unrelated to us, then nobody is hurting. The pain still exists but it is outside the ego, somewhere "there" as an object and can be tolerated easier.

BRAIN

The real relationship between brain and consciousness is different from practical concepts. Consciousness is not dependent on the brain and is not a product of the brain.

Persons who after brain stroke are not able to think, talk, or move have the same consciousness as before. Only the functions, that is manifestations, of their consciousness are altered; i.e their capability to speak, move, think, or perceive is limited because of the damage of the instrument of consciousness - the brain. Their capabilities are limited because of the damage to brain cells needed to perform these functions.

There is no seat of consciousness in the brain; therefore, we can remove any portion of the brain without removing consciousness. We can alter the content, functions, or ability of consciousness to respond to certain stimuli, to perceive, to act, etc. but we cannot remove consciousness by removing any particular brain cell.

Consciousness is present in the waking state, in dreams, in deep sleep, and in the "unconscious state" when we are not aware of anything. Because an average person is not able to remember the state of consciousness in deep sleep or during fainting, such states are considered to be unconscious. By certain yogic exercises described in this book and in some other books, it is possible to remember the state of empty, clear, lucid consciousness while in a deep sleep without dreams.

Aside of its other functions, the brain works as a machine for focusing attention to a particular limited sphere and for automatization of functions. Brain, with the help of memory, has a tendency to perform repeated tasks automatically.

First, brain enables the attention to concentrate on new or more important tasks and to focus on decision-making processes and on the use of will. Second, brain contains automatisms arranged upon each other from the beginning of functioning of the brain and ending with damage (dementia) or death. These automatisms are not static; they are repeating patterns of the same or of similar motions and are capable of influencing all functions of the brain at all times if triggered into activity by related signals. These automatisms relate all of our present experiences to past similar experiences, coloring them emotionally, adjusting intellectually and influencing our decisions and wants.

Brain is in consciousness and does not exist outside of consciousness. The whole body, including the brain, is an organ of consciousness and is an imagination, a creation of consciousness in the same way as the senses are.

THOUGHTS

Thoughts are very personal and differ from person to person to a great degree. The perceptions of one person share many similarities with the perceptions of other persons. Thoughts are imagined and usually controlled or influenced by our will. Perceptions are imagined involuntarily and usually are not controlled or influenced by our will. Thoughts are about 100 to 10,000 times weaker than perceptions. Thoughts are usually concepts, or dim auditory imaginations of words. Less often, they are dim visual or other imaginations. Imaginations of perceptions are keen, more precise, and qualitatively corresponding to a certain kind of senses. Both thoughts and perceptions are our imaginations.

Perceptions are usually altered by our concepts about the perceived objects - mainly by wants, wishes, expectations, emotions, and memory - thus, they are not exact and do not totally correspond with the perceived objects. Our perceptions are mainly influenced by desire to live and to have pleasurable feelings. If such concepts are entirely stopped and do not influence perceptions, then the reality, such as it is, can be perceived directly during the perceptions of objects.

EMOTIONS

Emotions are evoked by thoughts. Because thoughts are dependent on memory, emotions thus are triggered by memory. Emotions can be very deceptive and influence our decisions and behavior more than anything else - very often more than drives. Emotions are very subjective and range widely from lower and negative (i.e. selfish) ones to higher and positive (i.e. altruistic) ones. Positive social, ethical, and esthetic emotions are desirable for existence of every human community. The highest emtions are loving kindness, empathy, sympathy and desire to do good to other living beings and to help them. Higher emotions help us to feel the unity with other living beings and thus help us to induce the experience of realization.

PERSONALITY

We feel that we are a personality separate from others. Since the personality is a feeling, personality exists only in the consciousness and does not exist outside of the consciousness.

Consciousness is more than personality. Consciousness is impersonal and has two aspects: an unmanifested one and a manifested one. The manifested aspect is the universe.

The center of our personality is called ego. We refer to ego as "I" or me. The most important step toward realization is to realize that we are not a separate ego, we are more than ego, ego is only an imagination of the impersonal consciousness; and, in reality, we are this impersonal consciousness. When our entire personality, including ego feeling, disappears from our consciousness, our real being - consciousness itself - still remains and cannot be ever annihilated because it is not subjected to changes.

The feeling of personality disappears in deep sleep. Personality feeling can also disappear during psychological death, physical death, a certain kind of concentration, and realization of empty consciousness.

There is no reincarnation of personality or of ego. The body, personality, and feeling of ego are transitory, changeable, and temporary imaginings existing as unreal and impermanent. What is eternal and not dying is the unmanifested impersonal consciousness. This impersonal consciousness is unceasingly manifesting itself as the universe. It is changing from moment to moment, this means, it is dying and being reborn from moment to moment. All personalities with their individual universes originate from the same impersonal, spaceless, timeless consciousness. Consciousness is universal, not personal. Unmanifested consciousness itself was never born, will never die, and remains eternally the same.

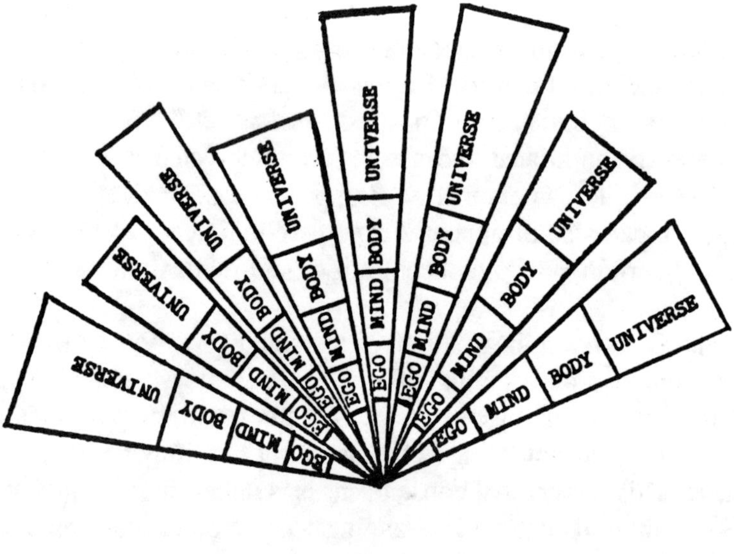

All personalities and personal worlds originate from the same timeless, spaceless, impersonal consciousness. On this picture, consciousness had to be illustrated as a point, although point is just a concept.

DRIVES

People are usually driven by wish for pleasure or fear of pain. A more powerful drive than the drive for pleasure is the drive for self-preservation. The most powerful drive, known so far, is the maternal drive for the preservation of progeny.

People usually do not want to die and wish a continuation of their personal lives after death of the body. They create beliefs in heaven, or paradise, and in eternal life as a separate soul. They believe in a god, or gods, and in rewards for good deeds and retaliation for bad deeds. Many believe that they are good and will go to heaven and that some other people are bad and will go to hell, especially if they harm others or if they do not control their sexual drives. Thus, they create religions. Others believe in reincarnation of their souls and in karmic justice - that every one of their deeds will have an effect on their future lives.

Everything that is believed is not true simply because of belief. Reality and truth do not need to be believed; they can be perceived directly and immediately. A belief, or faith are obstacles to the realization of truth.

The self-preservation drive is, indeed, an ego preservation drive. Intuitively we know that as consciousness we are immortal. But the self-preservation drive makes us project this intuition of immortality onto ego and believe in the immortality of ego. Some religions call this ego a soul. Indeed, ego and soul are only impermanent concepts. Everything that has arisen must perish because of being created and composed of something. No composed thing is permanent. Only that which was not born, not created, and which is not composed of anything will not die. Only that most simple substance is not involved in the birth-death play. There is no advantage in clinging to the unstable and identifying oneself with the impermanent.

If somebody wants to know the truth, his strongest drive should be a passion for truth, to know it and to live it. Desire to live is an obstacle to realization of truth. Similar obstacles on one hand are wanting, wishing, desiring, and hoping and on the other hand - fear, aversion, and resentment.

Objectivity, detachment from oneself, and non-biased views and deeds are the right attitudes. But loving kindness, compassion, and work for the well-being and realization of others are necessary because they are an antidote and counterbalance to the drive of selfishness.

At the beginning, the realization of pure consciousness can be temporarily attained by wanting it. However, realization cannot be maintained permanently by those who want it for themselves because pure consciousness is without wanting and selfishness and without feeling of personality.

MEMORY

Memory is an ability of consciousness to create present imaginations similar to former ones. Memory is a constantly repeating pattern of motions in the brain, similar to those which happened when the remembered thing was experienced. This is not a static deposition of something for storage, but is a constant similar movement. These patterns change at a much lower pace than other events; therefore, we feel that our memory is something stable and other things - like surroundings, body, feelings, emotions, and thoughts - are changeable and unstable.

Memory causes us to feel the continuity of ego. Because the ego feeling is relatively more stable than the changing events and feelings, we have an impression of identical and permanent ego. Indeed, even the ego feeling is changing and is not the same as it was several years ago.

Memory is not an exact recollection and is usually not reliable. Memory is a present imagination patterned after other imaginations that have happened before in our consciousness.

Memory is the cause of desire and fear, of wanting and aversion, and of anger and attachment. Memory influences and distorts perception of the present reality and can interfere with awareness of the unity of consciousness.

TIME

Changes in our consciousness make us feel time. The concept of time helps us organize changes in our consciousness successively. The feeling of time is related to the rate of changes and to the emotional attitude toward happenings. The pleasant happenings pass quickly, and the unpleasant ones drag slowly. Physical theories state that there are about 10^{43} happenings (changes) in one second.

Where there is no change, there is no time. Pure consciousness is without change. Therefore, it is without time. Beyond time, there is only eternal now.

The time of which we are conscious is only in our consciousness. Consciousness itself is not in time, is not subjected to time, and is beyond time. Consciousness is more than time. Consciousness creates time from itself, and time is only its imagination.

Objective time, i.e. time outside of consciousness, is only a theory created by the consciousness. Nothing can happen outside of the consciousness because time and happenings can exist only in the consciousness. Without time, i.e. without change, nothing can exist except eternal consciousness itself. Consciousness can exist without time, but time cannot exist without consciousness.

The past does not exist. The past is only a present imagination about other imaginations that existed as present ones in the consciousness. The future, also, does not exist. The future is only a present concept in the consciousness about changes which we are now supposing will happen after the present state of consciousness. Past and future are just present concepts.

There is no past and no future. There is only a constant change of the state of consciousness in the eternal "now" in the ever present consciousness. There is no beginning and no end of consciousness.

SPACE

To differentiate one thing from another, and to become conscious of more than one object, one must create space. Where there is no space, there cannot exist two or more objects. Where there is only one thing, there is no space. Space can exist only when there are two or more things.

The space, of which we are aware, is only in our consciousness. We cannot say that our consciousness is in space because space is just one of its manifestations. Consciousness can exist without space. Space cannot exist without consciousness. Consciousness creates space of itself in order to locate its manifestations into this space, to differentiate them, and to organize them.

Consciousness is as large as the space of which it is conscious at that given time. Consciousness is present wherever there are objects of which it is conscious.

Where there are objects, there is an observer. Where there is an observer, there are objects. Where there is no observer, there are no objects. Where there are no objects, there is no observer; but there is still pure consciousness itself. Existence of objects or observer depends on consciousness. Existence of consciousness does not depend on objects.

What is true about observer, observation, and the observed object is also true about thinker, thinking, and thought. Where there is a thought, there is a thinker. Where there is a thinker, there is a thought. Where there is no thought, there is no thinker. Where there is no thinker, there is no thought.

Likewise, where there is no time, there is no space. Where there is no space, there is no time. But there is still consciousness itself. Empty space does not equal empty consciousness. Empty consciousness is without space and not in space.

According to physics the shortest space unit (distance) is about 10^{-33} of a centimeter. Nothing smaller than this can exist. Paradoxically, one ccm of empty space has more energy than all the objects in the whole universe: about 10^{84} joules. This is because objects are a diluted, deformed, vibrating space. Space is a manifested (spread out, laid out, diluted, displayed) consciousness. Space has greater density than objects, and consciousness has infinite density. Empty, spaceless consciousness also has infinite energy because it creates universes, one after another, of itself.

We cannot become aware of any space outside of our consciousness. We never have been able to and never will be able to prove that there is any objective space outside of consciousness. Space is created only in consciousness. There is no space beyond consciousness; and, therefore, there are no subjects and no objects, no observer, and nothing observed outside consciousness. Nothing can exist outside of consciousness because there is no space for any existence.

The speed of light is the same for every observer (measurer) because there is only subjective space and time and there are only subjective universes. There is no objective universe independent of consciousness.

Empty consciousness becomes manifested in such a way that it becomes a universe; it radiates a universe of itself; it changes itself into a universe. The universe then disappears back into empty consciousness.

Any theory that there exists another cosmic, god's, or any other consciousness outside of or separate from our present consciousness is only a theory - a thought created in consciousness and from the substance of consciousness. This substance is not in space, not in time, and is not composed of anything, is simple, inexhaustible, timeless, and eternal.

In reality, "there" does not exist because everything is able to exist only "here" in consciousness, inside of consciousness. "There" is just a present concept in consciousness.

Pure, empty consciousness without objects is spaceless. Without space, only unmanifested, latent, eternal consciousness exists.

DIRECT EXPERIENCE VERSUS THEORIES

We can doubt our knowing and knowledge because of distortions created by past experience, fallacies caused by concepts, emotional colorings, illusions caused by suggestions and expectations, and contradiction of ego (me) and things (not me). However, the direct experience itself, existing in our consciousness at the present moment, cannot be doubted.

States of consciousness (experiences of which we are conscious now) must exist in such a way as they are experienced, no matter if they are - according to our or other's judgement - distorted, changed, modified, or imagined differently by the mind. Interpretations can be different, but the momentary state of consciousness, as it is experienced, is a fact. The state of consciousness, as it exists now, is a fact.

We directly experience our perceptions, feelings, and thoughts. We are aware of them directly. Independent matter is only a concept, a theory, deduced by practical thinking from our perceptions and feelings.

We can explain the unknown by the known, but to try to explain the known by the unknown can be absurd. Therefore, it is a mistake to explain our direct experience in our consciousness by materialistic theories. Such explanations are a denial of facts in our consciousness. They are an acceptance of theories as though they were facts. Today's science is not, and will not be, able to successfully explain what is mind or consciousness by materialistic theories and predicaments about non-living matter. Physical theories about material particles sometime end up in absurdities.

We know and experience our consciousness and its manifestations directly, but we never experience and know matter directly. Therefore, matter will forever remain only a theory. We cannot explain consciousness in terms of matter; yet, we can explain matter only in terms of consciousness. All theories, including the materialistic and idealistic (mental) ones, are only imaginations of our consciousness. Because of this no theory, whatsoever, is the Ultimate Reality or Truth.

Once more: the existence of consciousness explains not only its own existence, but also the existence of objects and the existence of theories about objects. On the other hand, attempts to explain consciousness with the help of materialistic theories will remain impossible forever.

NON-DUALISM

Where there is an object, there must be a subject, and vice versa. Where there is a figure, there must be a background. Every organism depends on its environment, is influenced by it, and influences it. Every thing exists in the field surrounding it. Every movement has a non-moving background. Even the smallest particle interacts within the system of which it is a part and undergoes transformations under the influence of that system. Things are interdependent and influence each other, as well as being influenced by each other. The observer and the observed are dependent on each other and influence each other mutually. There are no totally isolated objects or happenings. The whole universe is a unity. Every object and subject is a unity with the universe because

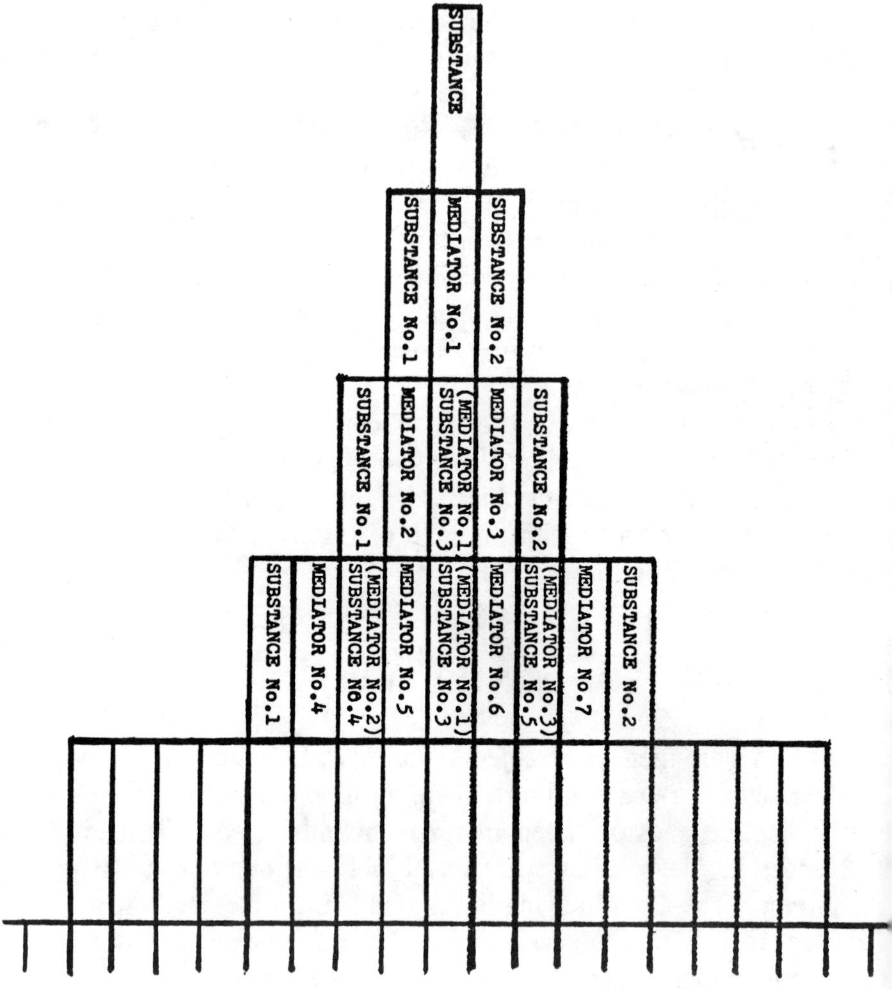

Dualistic and pluralistic theories about substance are logically absurd

everything is made of consciousness and cannot be separated from it. The only exception is pure, empty consciousness - without anything in it. It can exist by itself because it is not a creation and not an object or a subject.

There exists only one substance of which the universe is composed. If there were two different substances, then there would be a need for something that would unify them and serve as a mediator between these two substances. Otherwise, they would not be able to exert any influence on each other, nor would they know about the existence of each other. Thus, two different substances postulate an existence of a third substance functioning as a mediator. Now, we again have the same problem, but, instead of two substances, we have to solve the interaction between three substances. These three substances, again, require two or three mediators which in turn become new substances. This situation means that we now have to postulate five or six substances and a number of mediators. This way of thinking can continue indefinitely, or we can conclude that the universe cannot be explained in this way and that we have to accept its unity.

Physics, as well as metaphysics, is searching for Grand Unified Theory of the universe and it's energies. The universe and consciousness can be understood only if we accept them as a unity. Everything is only one consciousness that has two aspects - an unmanifested and a manifested one.

Although consciousness can be explained as a unity, it cannot be experienced, perceived and lived as such by thinking - that is, by concepts and theories. Concepts interfere with the experience of the ultimate truth.

SUBSTANCE

The substance of which the universe is composed has been called matter, god, consciousness, mind, being, self, life, soul, spirit, nature, etc. The substance we know directly and experience directly is the substance of which our perceptions, imaginations, feelings, emotions, thoughts, and concepts are built. This substance is our consciousness. Products of our consciousness are experienced directly as a first-hand experience. Therefore, we should prefer the term "consciousness" or any mental term (symbol) when explaining the substance (or basis) of the universe and of ourselves. Whatever cannot be experienced directly and known without a mediator, for example, matter, god, nature, soul, spirit, etc. is an improper symbol. Such terms will forever remain only a theory - more or less probable - but never a fact and never above doubt.

The substance of consciousness is the same as the substance of the body and of other objects in the world. Objects can influence the body and consciousness. Consciousness can influence the body and, by help of the body, also objects. The substance of consciousness has to be the same as the substance of the mind, body, and objects; otherwise, they would not be able to influence each other. Consciousness is the substance of everything.

Seemingly opposite things, like white and black, sound and silence, thoughts and objects, are not two different substances. They are just two phases - two different manifestations - of the same one substance.

Materialistic theory was derived from physical experiments, but this theory has been unable to explain basic facts in the universe and consciousness. Experiments to prove the existence of non-living matter composed of subatomic particles, so far, has brought physics and its metaphysics to absurd contradictions. Materialistic theory has been subjected to changes and is being replaced by new theories able to explain both the universe and consciousness. What we believe to be a non-thinking and non-living matter is, indeed, a living intelligent consciousness.

The substance of consciousness is not born and does not die, does not come from somewhere and does not go anywhere, does not change with time, and does not become something else. It cannot be killed, annihilated, or removed. This substance is eternal, alive, intelligent, sacred, and always present here and now. This is our pure, empty, unmanifested consciousness.

THE WAY OF SCIENCE

According to the present science, material objects are composed of molecules, and molecules are composed of atoms. Atoms are composed of particles, i.e., electrons, protons, and neutrons. These, in turn, are composed of quarks and gluons, and these of strings. Logically the next step after strings should be some sort of dots or points, but in the present atomic physics it is not.

Particles are composed of energy, i.e., are a form of energy. Energy moves in waves. According to the atomic physics particles are patterns of standing energy waves. Energy is a cause of change or movement. Cause is a mental category, a concept, a thought. A concept is an imagination of consciousness, a product of consciousness. Consciousness is something that cannot be defined or described without using the same term in its definition either apparently or in concealment. Consciousness cannot be reduced to anything more basic. We cannot get beyond consciousness. Scientific concepts thus are bringing us from objects to consciousness. Quantum theory of physics requires existence of an observer and thus requires existence of living consciousness.

The laws of the universe will not be changed by replacing the concept of matter with the concept of consciousness. Universal laws will be working the same way, and we must respect them even after we have understood that everything is consciousness. But we will understand them and use them better.

Particle theory has many contradictions. For example, if a material particle occupies a space (or plane or line), it has to be composed of something and be further divisible. Only an abstract point does not occupy space. However if the last particle is a point and does not occupy space, it cannot be seen or otherwise found because no matter would be firm. Therefore, it would not be casting shadow or reflecting energy waves. Even compositions of such particles could not have different properties than one such particle and could not be registered.

Today, atomic physics has many other problems. One example of such problems is the behavior of light. At one time light behaves like a particle, and at another time like a wave. Therefore, physics is beginning to replace the theory about existence of matter and particles with theories about relationships between manifestations (happenings). Quantum mechanics is a study of correlations between experiences. The universe is beginning to be viewed not as a dummy mechanism or an unconscious machine, but as a living, conscious, intelligent, interrelated organism.

Presently, there are two scientific ways how to know the substance of which the universe, our bodies, personalities, imaginations, and thoughts are made. The first way is subatomic physics - to split the atoms in order to find the substance. This way is personally available only to those having access to instruments for fission of atoms. Moreover, it does not enable the person to directly see the particles or the substance itself. They will be seen only with help of instruments. Thus, the physicists can only create a theory (concept, thought) about the substance. This way they are able to know only their own thoughts about the substance and never the substance itself.

The second scientific way is to find the substance of which our mind, thoughts, emotions and imaginations are made. This requires experiments with one's own mind. This is the way to know the substance without an outside instrument. Here the substance of which everything is made is experienced directly without a mediator (instrument). Such realization of the basis of consciousness is experienced the same way by everybody even though it can be called by different names and described from different viewpoints. This second way is available to everybody and, moreover, not in an unknown future, but here and now. It is done by specific meditation techniques. Some of these techniques are described in the second part of this book.

LIFE

Life is change and reproduction. Life - as well as consciousness, time, space, change, and causality - is inherent and innate in the universe. The whole universe is alive. Even a stone has consciousness and life, although very simple, because there are constant unceasing changes and movements in the stone. Nothing unconscious can beget anything conscious, and nothing conscious can beget anything unconscious. This means that something unconscious does not exist.

Objects can differ as to form, content, reactivity, and other functions; but they can never become unconscious or nonliving, even for a moment. Everything lives a more or less complicated life - from the largest conglomerate of living cells to the tiniest physical particle. Organic life differs from the inorganic mainly by the ability to reproduce itself.

Birth and death are opposites. They are milestones in an uninterrupted process of life. Life is eternal and has no opposite or contradiction.

CONSCIOUSNESS

The term consciousness, in this book, has a meaning different from current concepts. Consciousness has two aspects: an unmanifested and a manifested one. The unmanifested, state-free aspect is the immobile source, origin, basis, and substance of the manifested aspect. The manifested aspect is the states of consciousness which we know as things, space, time, personality, feelings, emotions, thoughts, imaginations - in short, the universe.

The universe is created of consciousness and dissolves in consciousness. Consciousness is more than the universe. Universe is only a manifested aspect of consciousness.

Consciousness is the thinker, thinking, and the thought; the feeler, feeling, and the feelings; the observer, observation, and the observed; the witness of the drama of the universe, witnessing and, also, that drama itself. Consciousness is the creator creating things of itself like an amoeba taking numberless shapes on itself, or like a chameleon taking a variety of colors so that it cannot be easily recognized in nature, or like a cinema screen on which images of the universe are projected. Consciousness is the imaginer forming imaginations from and for itself - like a living dough forming itself consciously into numberless shapes.

Empty consciousness has no shape. The unmanifested aspect of consciousness is without any content. It is objectless, spaceless, timeless, impersonal, and not caused. Further, it is simple, not composed of anything, alive, intelligent, and sacred. Yet, it is infinitely more real than it's manifested aspect. Compared to the unmanifested aspect, the universe is only like a dream, a magic apparition, a moon's reflection on water, a shadow, a smoke form, a ghost, a hologram, a mirage, an echo, a phantasm, a rainbow, or a reflection in a mirror.

When we want to stress that the unmanifested aspect of consciousness is beyond contradictions, we call it pure being. Being, in our imagination, has no opposite because non-being does not exist, and we cannot imagine non-being.

Unmanifested consciousness does not have any attributes. All statements about unmanifested consciousness can be ultimately negated because statements belong to the sphere of thinking, of manifestation. Every intellectual activity is limited to the manifested, phenomenal existence. Unmanifested, noumenal being is

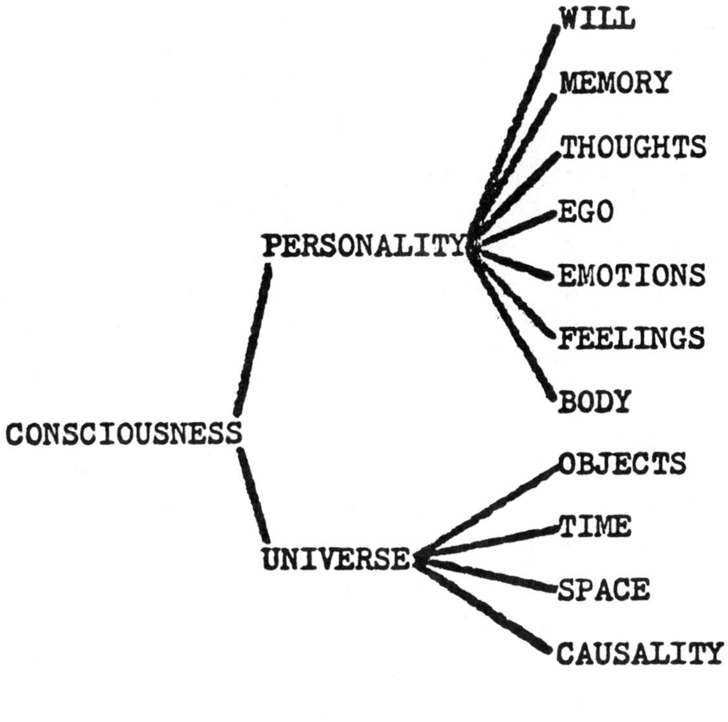

Everything is made of consciousness

out of comprehension of thinking intellect. Unmanifested being can be thought of only negatively - that is to say it is not this or not that. We cannot say that consciousness is this or that because once we make a statemnt, this statement is already a manifestation of consciousness. Indeed unmanifested consciousness only IS. There is no experience of existence or non-existence or any other experience in it.

Unmanifested consciousness can be realized for only a "timeless period" as it is beyond time, without time. It cannot remain isolated as there is no time for duration; it must become manifested again immediately.

Unmanifested consciousness cannot become aware of anything because, if it did, then there would be the one who is aware, the awareness, and an object of awareness. Therefore, when one realizes that state and then gets back into the manifested state of consciousness, one cannot say how long it lasted. This always seems to be just a fraction of a moment even though many hours have elapsed, for example, during a deep sleep. The minimal period during which one can be in the state of empty consciousness itself is the time between two happenings, two sucessive changes of consciousness. According to physics that could be approximately 10^{-43} of a second.

Once someone has realized empty consciousness itself, there is a possibility of keeping the awareness of it, along with the manifested aspect, during regular activities in the world.

FOURTH STATE OF CONSCIOUSNESS

There are three commonly known states of consciousness: waking, dreaming and sleeping. The fourth state of consciousness is the basis of all states of consciousness. This is the highest, most intensive and most real state of consciousness. Awareness of this fourth state can be realized as pure, empty consciousness; or this state of consciousness can be maintained together with the above three common states of consciousness. The fourth state of consciousness gives unlimited rest and relaxation to the mind, makes it free, enables it to think impersonally and realistically, and enables the mind to see situations objectively and to act correctly.

The fourth state of consciousness is the unmanifested state of consciousness and is the basis, source, beginning and end of everything.

WHY VERSUS HOW

The only explanation of "why" is the act of will. Explanation of everything else is an explanation of "how" not of why. Pure consciousness can only be. Pure consciousness is not aware of anything and is static. To be aware of anything requires an act of will. By an act of will, consciousness reflects itself in its creations. Thus, static consciousness becomes dynamic.

Consciousness divides itself into a subject (that which is conscious), and into objects (that of which it is conscious) by an act of its will (that means by wanting to do it). Thus, consciousness can perceive itself as reflected in objects, like in a mirror.

By developing a body and senses, consciousness also develops a thought of ego and of a separate personality; and it identifies itself with these. Then, consciousness regards objects and universe not as itself but as something different from itself.

The way back from manifestations and happenings to pure, empty consciousness is to not want anything (nor want to not want anything), to be content with quietude and tranquility, and to be that quietude and tranquility.

DIALECTICS OF UNIVERSAL ILLUSION

The basic function of consciousness is creating imaginations. Several steps are involved in this process: first, consciousness creates opposites; for example, white-black, sound-silence, firm-mobile, pleasure-pain, good-evil etc. The second step consciousness takes is making a contrast between "I" and not "I" - this means, a contrast between me and the universe. The third step is the identification of the feeling of "I" with the body. The attention becomes limited to sensory organs of the body. Here begins the illusion that we are just this body and continues, also, with the contrast between personality and the universe.

The fourth step is the differentiation between perceptions of objects and between thoughts, emotions, and imaginations. At this step, we attach the feeling of reality to perceptions because perceptions are not subjected to our will, especially if they are objects that change so slowly that we do not perceive their change. Here is the beginning of illusion about the unchangeable matter. Indeed, the perceived unchangeable reality is the substance of our consciousness; it is not matter.

We pay so much attention to our imaginations that we forget what we really are. Thus, the illusion about body, personality, and matter is completed.

The cause of the self deception about oneself and the universe is selfishness and the wish to feel happy now and after the death of the body. In this way, consciousness is split into a personality and into the rest of the world. Personality fights with the whole world for its self-preservation and pleasures. This battle of selfish personalities is the cause of suffering.

If somebody does not make any difference between himself and the world, then he does not create a difference between "I" and "not I," between subject and object. Thus, unselfishness helps one to be conscious of the universe in the right way and to again become aware of the unity of consciousness. Return to the unity of consciousness, when we are aware of being the whole universe and not just a separate personality, can solve ethical problems and remove suffering much better than any laws or religions.

KARMA: THE LAW OF CAUSE AND EFFECT

Karma is a theory assuming the existence of the law of cause and effect. It is a tendency of the consciousness to imagine similar things in a similar way as it has done before.

Repetition of the same deeds or happenings leads to a habit. Habit repeated innumerable times becomes a law of nature. Karma then is a common name for memory, motivation, habit, fate, and the laws of nature. It is an innate characteristic of the mind. The mind is under the influence of its karma. Unmanifested consciousness is not under the influence of karma.

Karma is fourfold:

Immediate: whatever we do - good or bad or neutral - we do it to ourselves as we are the whole universe.

Reactive: deeds of our personality influence the actions of other beings toward us and, thus, our deeds will be repaid to us according to our motivations and our deeds. The world will become better or worse as a result of our deeds and of the reactions of others to our deeds. What we are sowing now, we will be reaping in the future and, if not us personally, our descendants will reap it.

Habit forming: whatever we do or think causes development and strengthening of habits. Habits influence our future actions and cause future karma. Thus, every repeated thought and motivation is improving or damaging our mind according to the quality of our thinking and motivation resulting in deeds.

Hereditary (transferred by genes): because our tendencies to act in a certain way are hereditary, our offsprings will often in many aspects act the same way as we do. Thus, our actions will be repaid to us by our children during our old age. Because our children are a continuation of our genes, sometimes they can reap our karma.

Aside from the individual karma, there exist karmas of families, and groups. For example, there are racial, national, human, and planetary karmas as well as karmas of any other groups of beings.

SEMANTICS

The science of verbal communication indicates that different words can have the same meaning and that the same word can have different meanings. This influences the communication of knowledge and understanding from one person to another.

Aside from imperfections of language, a different understanding of the meaning of statements can be caused by different associations of that particular person. These different associations are caused by different experiences and perceptions connected with that word. The understanding also is influenced by present thoughts, emotions, wants, expectations, and other attitudes. Further, quality of attention plays a big role. Therefore, communication of any statement is usually not an accurate one.

Abstract terms and ideas are communicated in a more distorted way than the concrete ones. Many words are just seemingly meaningful. Analysis of the possible meanings of terms used in metaphysics is, therefore, important. Many mystic and religious scripts are often considered as being poetry, though their authors meant the statements literally.

No matter how clear the sentences are in this book, they will be understood differently by different people. Only the realization of the unity of consciousness will ultimately give the same meaning of the term "realization" to everyone. Without realization of pure, empty consciousness, nobody can know what empty consciousness is. A word is not the thing, an idea is not the reality. Unity of consciousness and empty consciousness are not ideas to be understood, but states of consciousness to be realized. Empty consciousness is our real, basic being and cannot be realized just by the understanding of ideas. Ideas and understandings are products of consciousness and, therefore, they veil the Ultimate Truth and divert attention from reality. To philosophize about empty consciousness without a direct experience of it and without insight into it is similar to threshing empty straw - it will not bring the desired effect. As long as we have only ideas about empty consciousness, we have not realized it. Thinking cannot comprehend the ultimate truth. In addition to imperfections of language, the fallacies, traps and imperfections of thinking, feeling, rearing, education, and environmental influences are like hypnotic spells preventing us from seeing the truth directly.

Some gurus try to keep teachings secret saying that they do not want to confuse the student. However, even the most open teaching about the realization will remain secret for those who have not had the experience of the unity of consciousness and of empty consciousness. The most they can do is to learn by heart the important sentences, but even after that, they will not understand their full meaning.

In tantras, the explanation of teaching is done by parables and metaphors. Those who are not yet ready for the teaching will not understand them. Meditators also use parables and stories during the persecution by organized religions or by the state. For example, tantras state that Bodhgaya, the place where Buddha attained realization, will not perish even if the whole universe perishes. Because Buddha attained realization under a fig tree, Buddhist pilgrims pray to that tree and believe that the fig tree will not perish. Indeed, Buddha attained realization in his unmanifested consciousness, and it is the unmanifested consciousness that will not perish even if the whole universe perishes.

Christ referred a parable about people from the street invited to a wedding who did not have a white dress, and were thrown back onto the street. White dress meant here empty consciousness, and wedding meant realization of the unity of

What is an elephant?

Five blind persons were arguing about what an elephant was. The first one said: It is like a spear. The second one said: It is like a snake. The third one said: It is like a wall. The fourth one said: It is like a trunk of a tree. The fifth one said: It is like a broom.

consciousness. If anybody gets realization but is not able to keep his mind free of concepts, he will lose it.

CONCEPTS

Everything appearing in our consciousness, everything that we become aware of, is a concept. Ego and objects, personality and universe, matter and mind, substance and form, wisdom and ignorance, unity and multiplicity, god and devil, heaven and hell, faith and disbelief, time and space, etc. are concepts.

Concepts can be correct or incorrect; but they are just thoughts, imaginations of consciousness. Also, the correct concepts about the unity of consciousness or about empty consciousness are just thoughts - that is, manifestations of consciousness but not the consciousness itself.

Concepts keep us in illusion and confusion and deceive us. They make us err and act inappropriately. If we want to realize pure consciousness, we have to leave all concepts behind. Consciousness cannot be comprehended or understood by concepts - this means, by thinking about it. Consciousness can be realized only when we quiet the mind. When the mind becomes relaxed, indifferent and detached the concepts cease by themselves.

Every being perceives the universe in a different way, not only because of different sensory organs, but also because of different concepts. Concepts of every being differ by past experience, memory, wanting, expectations, fears, associations, views, etc.

When we do not have concepts, we see objects the way they are and the situation as it really is. This helps us to act appropriately. Finally, all concepts, good and bad, interfere with empty consciousness.

If we have concepts, then the concepts should be good and altruistic ones. All the concepts, good or bad, that enter our consciousness are not harmful as long as they are not followed and elaborated by our attention. To put it differently, we should not forget ourselves in them.

When we observe our mind, we should look at the concepts objectively and indifferently. We should try to see where they come from, where they disappear, and of what material they are made. Then, the concepts calm down by themselves, and we will not be influenced by them. After some time of assuming an objective, indifferent, and detached attitude toward concepts, they cease arising by themselves.

When all understanding, cognizing, thinking, imagining, and feeling quiet down and cease, there will remain immobile, tranquil, empty consciousness without concepts. This is the basis of everything - total peace, inactivity, relaxation and rest. This is the state behind thinking, understanding, and concepts. This state is a source and foundation of everything and can be realized only by doing absolutely nothing. However, this is not a dull state, but a state of immense intelligence without limits. Attention is there - as sharp as a blade.

When all concepts disappear, the thinker thinking concepts disappears with them. Wanting, searching, and understanding are also concepts.Therefore, this state of empty consciousness cannot be attained by wanting it, searching for it, or by understanding it. It can be realized by silence of thoughts, relaxation, ceasing of wanting and searching, and by stopping the effort to understand it.

REALIZATION

Realization of the unity of consciousness happens at once, like lightning. Suddenly, we recall what we really are. Attention becomes sharp and concentrated, and intelligence without limits appears.

We see that we are not a personality, personality is not real, and personality exists only as an imagination - a concept. We realize that only everlasting consciousness exists and that the body is just an imagination of that consciousness.

We know that our real being is this consciousness, that this consciousness was never born and will never die; it is eternal. All fears of death are utterly gone. We do not mind having the body die because, as consciousness, we cannot die. The body is just like a dress - we put away the old one and take on a new one.

We see directly that the whole universe is only an imaginary penomenon being costantly created by consciousness and dissolving unceasingly in it. Time is only an imagination of consciousness; consciousness is creating time. Space is, also, an imagination of consciousness; consciousness is creating space. Because we are this consciousness, space and time radiate from us. Space and time are only phenomena created by us. All perceptions are just our imaginations. The material of which everything is built is us.

We wake up at once to the Ultimate Basic Reality. Our senses become very keen - this is like waking suddenly from a dim dream to a beautiful sunny day. So great, and even greater is the difference in the clarity of our perceptions, thinking, and comprehension. Our consciousness is experiencing the Ultimate Reality and the basis of the universe. Nothing matters except that basic reality, because everything is It; everything is one. When the emotions and thoughts appear, they are entirely clear. There is a real freedom from everything.

Everything exists only in consciousness, and there is nothing that could exist outside of consciousness. Only consciousness exists, nothing else. Our ego was just a thought, a concept, and it disappeared. Also the feeling of separateness from the universe disappeared together with that ego.

Everything that could be accomplished has been accomplished. Consciousness posseses everything, and there exists nothing greater to wish, want, or need. Our own consciousness is that for which we have been searching, and it is the final goal.

We act unselfishly, because everybody and everything are we, ourselves. Selfish motivation would bring us back to the illusion that we are just a personality separated from the world.

When we fall asleep, we will be in a state of clear emptiness and will not lose consciousness. We cannot lose that state because it is the very basis of our existence. We can only again forget what we really are.

When we know our entire mind and all its workings, we will learn how to maintain that state of consciousness permanently or become aware of it whenever we want.

EMPTINESS

When we achieve an awareness of the unity of consciousness, we feel that nothing higher exists and that we have arrived at the goal. This is true concerning the way of perceiving the manifested consciousness; this means perceiving the universe in that state.

However, another still higher state of consciousness, above which nothing more is possible, exists. This conscious state of emptiness has no universe, no person, no time, and no space and is comparable to an empty timeless moment. The easiest time to accomplish the realization of this emptiness is when we are in the realization of the unity of consciousness. Emptiness can be realized in such a way that we change the whole content of consciousness (universe) into light. Then we concentrate and shrink that light together with space into one point. After this, we let go of that point and keep the concentration. Consciousness then becomes empty by itself. Because the spaceless emptiness is a higher state than the state of the unity of consciousness, consciousness returns from emptiness to the unity of consciousness. So, when we do concentration into one point of light without being in the realization of the unity of consciousness, we can bring about the realization of that unity.

We should not meditate on emptiness, as though emptiness were an object of meditation. Rather, we should keep the mind concentrated without an object until it becomes immobile, solid, firm, empty, silent, and quiet. But if we are accustomed to meditating on emptiness and our concentration is strong and without movement, then we should shrink the empty space into one point and subsequently let go of that point.

NEW STANDPOINT

A standpoint is a position or situation in which we really are. A viewpoint is a position or situation we only think of; we imagine it.

It is difficult to be unselfish without being in the state of realization of the unity of consciousness because only during realization we can see the nonexistence of reality of ourselves. Even if we logically conclude that we are consciousness and that being consciousness we are everything, without realization of the unity of consciousness we do not feel it and do not see it. Therefore, for such a person unity of consciousness is only a viewpoint, a new theory and not a new standpoint; this means, it is not a reality for him or her.

During realization there arises a direct, immediate perception that ego, or "I" does not exist really, that it is only an impermanent imagination. When we see the unreal existence of ourselves and of the entire phenomenal universe, then our consciousness becomes immediately filled with unlimited compassionate love for those beings that are unable to see the truth of unreal, impermanent existence of their phenomenal selves, and for this reason they suffer endlessly.

Thus the realization of unity of consciousness will place us at a new standpoint. We will not only understand but also will feel, and directly perceive the unity of us and the universe and that the universe is us, and we are the universe. This will be felt literally and really, not just as an idea or imagination. We are everybody and everything - every human being, animal, plant, mineral, and object. Consequently, we will treat everybody and everything as we do ourselves. We will be unable not to do so because we constantly see very clearly and feel that we are everything. Therefore, whatever we are doing to anybody and anything, we are doing it to ourselves. This is a new basis for our behavior.

ETHICS

Everybody, who has realized, does good to every living being and object unselfishly because his ethics have a new standpoint. He works for the elimination of pain and suffering from the life of all beings as well as he would from his own life. He does not do so because he believes, or because he has a personal, selfish interest in doing so, i.e. good reputation, glory, reward, praise, riches, friendship, good life, etc. He does so because he perceives and feels that the whole universe is his body; so by harming others, he harms himself; by helping others, he helps himself. He knows and feels that he is responsible for everybody and everything. His endeavor transcends his personal duties.

By understanding that wanting, resentment, sickness, death, and so on are just concepts, he develops love and compassion for everybody. This is not a sentimentality. Such love is counterbalanced by intelligence, reason, and understanding of truth. Right action requires wisdom and involvement of the whole personality, knowledge, experience, right motivation, etc.

Realization has to include and balance all of the main components of personality: intellect, emotions, will, and perceptions. The easiest one is the intellectual realization. One can get this by studying proper books, listening to the explanations of those having realization and, as a result, understanding that the basis of universe is consciousness and that we are consciousness. Yet, intellectual realization alone is not sufficient because without loving kindness, it is insensitive and arrogant. Without perceptual insight into the substance (reality), intellectual realization is empty.

Emotional realization can be obtained by loving kindness and compassion for everything and by treating all beings and objects like ourselves. Indeed, there is no permanent realization without loving kindness and compassion. However, emotional realization alone leads to silly and unrealistic behavior, moodiness, superstitions, and instability.

Will helps us to achieve realization through properly concentrating, controlling oneself, overcoming obstacles, maintaining rules and precepts, acting unselfishly, doing charity, and helping others to get realization. Yet, to cultivate only strong will and concentration alone can lead to forceful behavior, arrogance, fanaticism, and selfishness.

Perceptual realization can be obtained by mantras, by creating and dissolving visualizations, and by relaxation into absolute tranquility and stillness. Thus an insight into the substance of the universe will be obtained. Perceptual realization is the best of the previously mentioned ones; but, without an intellectual realization, it leads to superstitions, dogmatism, and fanaticism; without loving kindness and compassion, to recklesness; without will, to instability, isolationism and passivity. For these reasons, the best way to reach realization is through guidance of a realized Guru who knows the right methods and is able to correct our errors and personal shortcomings.

Everyone who lives the unity of consciousness lives the fullness of life and works for the fullness of life for others. That is he helps others, who are interested, become aware of the unity of consciousness. He does not do so by force because he highly values their freedom. He works for the elimination of basic ignorance and unnecessary suffering and for happiness, peace, and beauty of life. He is detached from the world, but not indifferent to the pain and suffering of others.

He works for peace and justice, but he is not weak or cowardly. After having exhausted all possible means to preserve peace, he will go to war and risk his limb and life if that is his duty. However, he must not wage a war for selfish reasons. He should do so without hatred, feeling of superiority, desire for power, or glory and riches. He should do it only as his duty and only to the extent necessary, without selfishness. He has to be ready to give up his position and power for higher reasons, for example, whenever it is in the common interest. Similarly, after having tried all possible means to correct a criminal, he will not hesitate to restrict or jail him, force him to work, and make him compensate for the harm caused to others - if this is his duty.

In dealing with others, the realized person applies understanding, tolerance, forbearance, forgiveness, sympathy, empathy, love, help, and charity because he knows this helps to diminish suffering. He respects opinions, philosophy, and religions of those who are striving for truth, but he does not yield to bigotry and fanaticism.

His sensitivity and understanding are far greater than that of an average person because his mind is entirely still, silent, immobile, impartial, and undistorted by wanting. He sees everything the way it really is. Undisturbed by wishes, prejudices, and emotions he is able to catch the finest nuances and shades in the thinking, feeling, wanting, and motivation of others.

Life becomes a great play for him. He knows and feels that he is that which cannot die. He does not cling to his personality which is only a transitory and perishable imagination and has to die sooner or later. He is aware that his body is just like a mask or a dress which, when worn out, will be put away and that everything created and manifested must die. Only that which is not created and unmanifested cannot die. Therefore, he does not become attached to the impermanent, but identifies himself with the eternal. He is free to act without being influenced by existential fears and egoistic desires. There is no more realistic attitude or correct ideology able to bring more good for the world or to make life better for all beings in the whole universe than the realization of the unity of consciousness. Without this unity even the best political system, religion, or organization of the human community will not bring desired heaven on earth. With this unity, even the worst systems or religions will improve the attitudes of people, and thus, bring about an improvement of life in this world. Nothing in personal or public life has such a great value as realization. This is the highest one can attain and do for others and himself. Therefore, the first and most important wish of those who have reached this state is to help others also attain it.

MEDITATIONS

MEDITATION EXERCISES

Realization, Enlightenment, knowing the Absolute, insight into Reality, Turyia Samadhi, Satori, Mahamudra, Zogchhen, etc., are different names for realizing the same unity of consciousness. This realization of the unity of consciousness can be inborn and thus it can happen by itself, or it can be induced by knowing oneself through realization of empty consciousness.

The means and ways to attain realization of the unity of consciousness may be fast or slow, temporary or permanent. They may include observation of one's mind, unselfishness, philosophical insight, constant awareness, stopping of the mind, concentration, indifference to oneself, detachment, devotion, love, compassion, faith, relaxation, reverie, creation and dissolution of imaginations, recollection exercises, magic rituals, mantras, ritual dancing, art impressions, tantric sex, some drugs, removal of perceptions, psychological death and impasse situation. They may include giving up one's personality, giving up wanting, surrendering to the highest intelligence, etc. All of these ways, however, most of the time induce just a temporary realization.

A permanent realization can be attained by objective observation of one's own mind. Knowing the working of the entire mind will bring the consciousness to silence, quietude, and emptiness. Even if self-discipline and meditations are necessary, realization cannot be accomplished only by forceful concentration or self-control. When climbing a mountain one has to use not only legs, but also hands and sometimes even teeth. Similarly, climbing the path to realization has to involve many methods at the same time. In the final stage, surrender to relaxation, rest with keen concentration, detachment from thoughts and imaginations, quietude, and immobility accompanied with a steady and even flow of concentration without an object are necessary. To accomplish that, we should follow great methods leading to tranquility, not small ones leading to activity. The best method is to follow instructions of a realized guru.

The goal of meditation exercises is to remove the feeling that we are just bodies or personalities and that the universe is real and different from us. From this viewpoint, we can divide meditation exercises into three groups.

The first group removes the feeling that we are the body and personality by removing the ego feeling. When the feeling of "I" is forgotten, the feeling of not "I" disappears. Then, objects are not separate from us. All is perceived and felt as an impersonal consciousness. The body is felt just as one of the objects in consciousness, but not as "I."

The second kind of exercise expands and identifies the ego feeling with the universe. Removing the feeling of independent objects and instilling the feeling that everything is in our consciousness and that we are everything eliminate the feeling of being a separate personality. It is similar to embracing the universe by consciousness. Everything is felt to exist in our suprapersonal consciousness.

The third approach is a simple negation of the difference between "I" and not "I." We deal with everything in the same way as with ourselves. We are constantly aware that the idea of "I," body, and the universe originates from our consciousness, changes in it, and dissolves in it. The only reality is the consciousness.

The most basic exercise is to constantly be aware that we are watching our own mind with our mind; the mind is observing itself. A constant awareness that everything is just a transient imagination - like a dream, a magic apparition, a moon's reflection on water, a mirage, a hologram, an echo, a phantasm, a rainbow, a or reflection in a mirror - is necessary.

The unity of consciousness is not something that one does not have, or that one is not. We always have been, and will be this unity. We just need to become aware of it and remember it constantly. Beacause we always are that unity, we can become aware of it right here in this very present moment. Only the iron habit of considering our real self as being only this body is preventing us from understanding and perceiving the unity. Therefore, meditation exercises are necessary.

PREREQUISITES FOR MEDITATION

The first important prerequisite for meditation is unselfish motivation. Selfishness increases the ego feeling and, thus, increases the separation of the person from the rest of the universe. Selfishness strengthens the concept of dualism and sets ego against non-ego, thus creating paranoia and preventing the realization of the unity of consciousness that can result from meditation.

The best motivation for meditations is to not want realization for oneself, but for all beings in the whole universe. The ideal should be buddhist boddhisattvas: they gave up their own realization for the sake of all beings and were doing meditation exercises to help others to reach their realization before they tried to reach their own. Wanting to be saved, liberated, enlightened, realized, reach heaven, eternal life, etc. for oneself is selfish and does not lead to realization. Even in a usual life selfishness causes struggling, fighting, suffering and, finally, spoils the best and most pleasant situations. We are the whole universe; therefore, we have to consider the whole universe first, and only then ourselves. Those who have love in their hearts for others, are able to sacrifice themselves unselfishly for others, ask nothing from life for themselves, or do not mind to die are closer to realization than those who want something for themselves.

It is necessary to prefer realization to anything else and to respect persons who reached it and hold them as an ideal. Those who prefer money, property, power, glory, pleasure, and fun will have difficulties to get realization. They are attached to the manifested universe and to their egos.

Detachment from the personality and the universe is the second important prerequisite to meditation. Realization requires giving up the universe, especially giving up the personal ego. The best way to give up our ego is to offer it for service to others with the idea that we are doing it to the highest consciousness of which everyone is a part. While performing a service to others we should remember that our personality, the performed service, and those to whom the service is given are all impermanent phenomenas - images in our mind.

Free time is a prerequisite to meditation. Many people who wanted to get realization but regarded their work and entertainment as being more important did not set aside time for meditations, and they died without realization. Free time for meditations is more important than entertainment. Those who have to work for a living, should acquire leisure time by lowering their material requirements. Thus, leisure time is another important prerequisite. Everyone can find some free time for meditations. We can meditate even while walking, eating, driving a car, before falling asleep, by waking up earlier than usual, during entertainment, etc. We should keep keen mindfulness all the time.

Obedience of the ethical and moral laws of the community is another minimal condition for the seeker. This allows a good conscience and a quiet, favorable environment free of persecution by others for being different. The ten Christian (Jewish) commandments, ten Buddhist commandments, or Muslim commandments, etc. have to be followed according to the community in which one is living. Of course, we should not adopt their false beliefs, superstitions, intolerance, or bigotry.

Having the right vocation is also important. Vocation should not harm living beings (for example, one must not be a butcher or fisherman), but should help others by one's work.

There are occasions when somebody is called to defend his or her own country as a soldier. If the cause for war is a just one, then one should take it as his duty. But, if possible, it is always better to avoid becoming a soldier and killing others.

Monasteries, cloisters, ashrams, etc. are not the right places for the realization of the unity of consciousness for several reasons. First, they prevent their members from having children thus making it impossible to transmit the hereditary disposition to realization to the next generation. Because of this, even the best religions degenerated and lost the ability to lead their believers to realization. Celibacy of the clergy causes degeneration of religion for the same reasons. Furthermore, the abbots without realization, competition of monks and nuns between themselves, rancor, homosexuality, unrealistic regulations, use of monks and nuns for unnecessary work, abuse of power, and other monasteric ailments can prevent realization. If one cannot avoid monasteries and similar institutions for a valid reason, then only old persons and persons with hereditary illnesses that make childbearing unwise may enter the monasteries for a long time, or permanently.

On the other hand, temporary retreats to solitary shelters and hermitages can be helpful. Attendance at organized meditation meetings for a short time - from several days to several months - is also useful to realization.

The most important prerequisite to realization is the desire to know the truth and to live it. Truth is first, advantage is secondary. Belief in pleasant self-deceptions, especially religious beliefs, are obstacles to the comprehension of truth. If something has to be believed, then it is not the truth. Truth can be known directly and immediately and does not require a belief or faith. Therefore, one should not be superstitious, credulous, and gullible. Uncertainity is better than a false belief. Belief and faith should be differentiated from trust. Trust in recommendations of a realized guru and willingness to try all his suggestions are correct attitudes.

BEHAVIOR

Behavior, feeling, and thoughts should be based on the highest ethics of realization, i.e., always being aware that we are also the other beings and objects, not just one personality. We are responsible for the whole world, because the world is us. Whatever we are doing to others, we are doing to ourselves. This is the reason why it was said that we should have compassion and love those who hate us, talk nicely about those who slander us, and do good to those who harm us. This is why it is better to get hurt than to hurt others. Of course, we have to use our own intelligence and avoid getting hurt by others. Evil cannot be removed by further evil, only by goodness. Therefore, we should not retaliate. Injustice done to our person should be born patiently. We have to understand that others are doing this to us because of their ignorance. But injustice done to others must not be tolerated and should be prevented or, if already happened, corrected. A malicious person is creating bad karma for himself and for the community where he lives, and should be prevented to do so, whenever possible.

It is necessary to have love and compassion, not only for living beings, but also for objects. We should not break or destroy objects for no good reason. Every object and place should be left in the same or better condition than when we found it. If we cannot avoid hurting somebody or something, we should choose the least possible evil. We should act from the viepoint of eternity. We have to act because the action is right, and not because of fear of consequences, hope or gain. At the same time we should be smart and use our intelligence. For example, indian sage Ramakrishna sent one of his students to a market to buy food. The student brought too little goods for the money he took with him. Ramakrishna asked him why he brought so little food. The student replied that saints do not bargain with farmers about the prices. Ramakrishna said: "You are not a saint, you are stupid."

We should always try to behave better than others, but let us not be arrogant - believing that we are better, or that we know more than others. We each have the same basic nature, even if we are not aware of it. We should not regard ourselves as chosen persons or people. The difference between a crazy person and a wise person is this: a crazy person thinks he is god or a chosen person and that others are devils and sinners, while a wise man sees the same divine nature in others as in himself.

Lying prevents realization. If we cannot tell the truth, then stay silent. The goal does not justify unfair means. Organizations and religions that permit the telling of lies or cheating under some circumstances "for a higher reason" destroy themselves because nobody can trust them. We should love truth and live by it.

The characteristics to cultivate in order to attain realization are unselfishness,charity, ethical behavior, contentment with what one has, independence, detachment, contentment with one's fate, tolerance, endurance, quiet mind, concentration, wisdom, intuition, and surrender to the highest intelligence of consciousness. Life has to be accepted as it is: painful and happy, boring and exciting, bad and good. It is necessary to stop wanting what we do not have and envying others. Nobody can be only happy and successful. Our success and happiness can come only at the expense of the success and happiness of others, and those others are, indeed, us. How can we be happy if others around us are unhappy? Therefore it is better to rejoice at the success and happiness of others than of ourselves.

Good is relative and depends on a viewpoint. If a cat eats a mouse, it is good or bad according to the viewpoint we assume. It is good for the cat and bad for the mouse. Therefore, we have to assume the widest and highest ethical viewpoint. Without a correct viewpoint, there is no permanent realization. Although our personal circumstances have shortcomings, this is still the best possible universe.

If something goes wrong, we do not look for mistakes of others and do not blame them. We should try to find where we did mistakes in handling the situation.

As we are everything, self-sacrifice is more correct than selfishness. When we cannot help somebody, we should at least wish to help him and imagine, during the day or during the dream, that we are helping him. Let us avoid causing negative emotions or pain to others and behave toward them in such a way as we wish them to behave toward us. Reckless behavior is an obstacle to realization. Our behavior should be an example for others as to how they can attain realization. A higher attitude is to treat others better than ourselves. The best possible attitude is to take on oneself the pain, unhappiness, and suffering of all living beings in the whole universe. Its important to wish them happiness and to do for them what they wish, but the first priority is to help them find the means to achieve realization. Even if doing this for the whole universe is possible only in our imagination, practically we have to do it for our closest environment.

Suicide, with one exception, is not right because it is selfishness and will prevent us from helping others. Also, consider the huge amount of non-human living beings that have no practical opportunity to attain realization. The probability to be born as a human being in this universe is very small. Quadrilions of quadrilions of microscopic living beings have to be born and eaten by each other and by larger animals in sewages, rivers, seas, ground, and in the air in order to enable the birth of one human being. Everybody has some suffering that needs to be endured. In an incurable disease there are pain medicines at our disposition. Only if this does not help can the sufferer decide to shorten his unnecessary suffering.

Many people do not tolerate views different from their own. Therefore, we have to keep our views and ideas in such company to ourselves and not talk about meditation and realization with those who have a negative attitude toward them.

We should not create religions, organizations, or groups because they separate us from others. This leads to conflicts. To attain the unity of consciousness, we should look for that which unites us, not which separates us.

TECHNICAL REMARKS

In order to meditate properly it is not necessary to believe the statements in sections about perception, time, space, etc., but it is necessary to understand them. If we do not understand them, it is necessary to study the subjects related to those statements thoroughly until we do understand them. We can think and create our own theories about those basic subjects. Nothing should be left unexplained.

If any little fact seems to be in contradiction with theories, we should not reject the fact; we should accept the fact, change the theories, and create such theories that are able to explain every fact. We should not adjust facts to the theories. Skepticism has to be carried to the very end. For example, we should not stop at the belief in eternal existence of soul or ego; we should not believe only in what we like and doubt only what we do not like. Especially, the common and traditional concepts accepted as obvious, self-explanatory, and true by society and that we have learned as a result of rearing and education should be doubted and analyzed.

The final goal is not the creation of newer and newer theories as life is too short; but to arrive at a solution and an understanding. The thinker finally has to be able to discard all thinking and conceptualizing because he has arrived at the basic solution or at its end because of an impasse. When he has understood that the thinking will not bring him any further, he will replace it by meditation exercises.

Before and after every meditation we should send to the whole universe in all dimensions a wish of love, compassion, happiness, peace, and realization to all beings. It is proper to imagine that we are taking other's sins and pains on ourselves in order to help them get realization effortlessly and easily. Such a prayer has to be repeated as a mantra as often as possible even when we are not sitting in a meditative position. The prayer can be as follows:

> **Loving kindness and compassion to the whole universe.**
> **Let well-being, happiness, and contentment prevail for all beings.**
> **I pledge to help all beings to realize the ultimate Truth.**
> **I am taking on the sins and pains of all beings, so that they attain realization of Truth without any effort.**

Some exercises have to be done by imagination and concentration - others, without any effort, by relaxation and rest. Everyone of them, however, has to involve the whole mind - entire consciousness. Therefore, it is good to imagine that the entire universe is meditating with us.

All meditations should be done with open eyes except meditations on recapitulation, sleep, and dream. We cannot see the Ultimate Reality with closed eyes.

After every meditation, we have to dedicate the progress and merits of meditation to the realization of the unity of consciousness of all beings in the universe. Then, we should relax and rest for a few minutes in the same position in which we meditated. The transition to activity has to be gradual so that we will be able to bring the attitude and quietude gained in meditation into the daily active life.

Great experiences, understandings, and insights into the reality or nature should not stop or divert us from the search for the Ultimate Truth. Every experience, no matter how sacred it seems to be, should be subjected to a thorough analysis after (but not during) the meditation. We should not feel sorry when it

Tibetan statue.
Insight into the Ultimate Reality is done with open eyes.

disappears. Everything - it must be emphasized - **everything** that appears in consciousness and then disappears is just an imagination and not the Ultimate Reality itself. We must not cling to it. The love for truth is more important than experiences and pleasant self-deceptions.

There are two categories of experiences in meditation. In the first one, there is an observer (experiencer) and the observed (experienced). This is a self-deception, because there is dualism. In the second one, the observer (experiencer) is at the same time the observed (experienced), and the observing. The observer does not feel different from the observed. Consciousness is a unity and, therefore, the second category of the states of consciousness is true. For example, we can feel and see the eternity which belongs to the first category. Or we can feel that we are the eternity itself - this belongs to the second category.

We should not look back at the past life and be proud of it or feel guilty about it. We should become aware of bad deeds, mistakes, and sins done in the past; regret them; undo them, if possible; and make a firm decision not to do them any more. After that, we should let go of such thoughts and feelings because negative thoughts and feelings interfere with meditation. Only the present attitude influences the meditation, not the past deeds. Therefore, it is right to do whatever we can to undo the past; and when we cannot do more, we should look at it as at a concept present in the mind. Then we should forget it and not brood over it. We have to live in the present and not in imaginations about the past or future.

The body has to be kept healthy, strong, and effective. We have to take care of the body as if it were a good horse needed to carry us and others to the realization. When we are sick and orthodox medicine cannot help us, then we should try unorthodox alternative treatments.

To meditate in the presence or under the guidance of somebody who has realization is better than to meditate alone. On the other hand, to be led by somebody who does not have realization is worse than to meditate alone. The one who had realization in the past, but is not having it presently can advise, but cannot lead. He cannot be regarded as a guru. Then the best guru is one's own consciousness.

When the first glimpse of realization disappears, we should not feel unhappy. Nobody can stand on his tiptoes for the rest of his life after the first try; similarly, nobody can have a permanent clear perception of reality for the rest of his life after the first experience of realization.

Reading and thinking about realization is like reading a prescription, and thinking about it. Just reading cannot help us. Only if we use the medicine, can it help us get cured. Similarly, only if we practice the meditation exercises, can we get cured from ignorance. We can then know the truth about ourselves, the universe, and the purpose of life.

BASIC MEDITATION

Basic meditation consists of being constantly aware that our personality, body, and the universe are just imaginations of our consciousness. Everything in our consciousness is just a waking dream, a concept. We should look at our personality objectively as though it were somebody else and stay detached from it.

This basic meditation should be done all the time, not just during rest, but also during activity. Along with this basic meditation, we can try all other meditation exercises in this book - one by one - each one of them for two to three months, and then adhere to those that help us the most.

After we will become aware of the part of consciousness that is non-moving, firm, and non-changing, then we should maintain this awareness all the time. This is clear, pure attention not directed at anything, that rests in itself, and is always present here and now. Mindfullness is the fastest way out of suffering. Whatever we are doing, we must remember to be mindful from moment to moment. Our worst enemies cannot harm us as much as our unguarded thoughts can.

If we had an experience of realization of the Ultimate Truth in the past, we should constantly maintain the attitude and insight we had during this experience. After the first realization, the first thought that comes to our mind is that we lost the seeing of reality. This thought makes us unhappy. This is a trick of mind to regain control over us. The reality is always present and cannot be lost. We can lose any object or any part of our body including our head, but we can never lose what is real because we are it. We should look at such negative thoughts, feelings, and at our own personality objectively - with indifference and detachment - and not believe such thoughts and feelings.

This basic reality is our customary, common, current everyday consciousness such as it is here at this present moment. Because we believe that we do not have this reality, we look for it. It is like looking for our own eyes. The moment we stop looking for it, quiet down, relax, cease thinking, wanting or rejecting anything, and look at once at the whole consciousness, seeing that all objects including the body, personality, emotions and thoughts are imaginations in the consciousness - at that moment we can see the reality again. Of course, such insight is weak and unstable at the beginning, but by constant maintenance of such standpoint and remembering it always, the realization of truth will strengthen and stabilize.

The basis of realization of truth is correct viewing of the world and correct standpoint. Therefore, it is important first to study and understand metaphysics of realization. On the basis of such understanding - that everything is just an imagination in consciousness - we can maintain the correct meditation. The second necessary thing is an alert, still, qiet, immobile and relaxed mind. Both - the correct view and tranquil mind - have to be trained and maintained. Remembering to maintain them is mindfullness.

The body should be relaxed and the attention alert, mindful. Attention has to embrace the whole consciousness. Nothing should be removed and nothing sought. Nothing should be refused and nothing should be wanted. Nothing should be judged as good or bad. Everything is right the way it is. We should keep our mind in constant awareness of that which is - from moment to moment.

Thoughts and emotions, be they negative or positive, cover the nature of consciousness and cause disturbance. They are naturally arising and disappearing from moment to moment. Do not touch them; do not follow them. Do not get attached to them. Let them be. By fighting thoughts or emotions, they become stronger. If we cannot pacify thoughts by mantras, then it is better to concentrate on them and thus become more aware of them. This way thoughts and emotions will dissolve by themselves automatically.

CONCENTRATION

The main door to realization is concentration of attention. Concentration can be done with an object or without an object.

During concentration on an object, we have to totally eliminate any thoughts and feelings not related to that object. We must just perceive the object. If we concentrate on an imaginary object or thought, then we have to imagine only that object or thought. The attention must be stable and evenly flowing. As an object, we can choose anything positive and interesting to us, be it a perception like the light of a candle, bodily feeling, emotion, thought, imagination, etc. Concentration on an object is of two types.

The first type of concentration is a dissolving one. At the beginning, an observer, observation (i.e., concentration), and the thing observed exist. Later, when the concentration becomes intensive, the object of concentration begins to dissolve. Keenly observed objects finally dissolve into the clarity of empty consciousness. This type of concentration is called Samadhi. Samadhi type of concentration should be one pointed, evenly flowing, clear, tranquil, steadfast, objective, and indifferent; this means with a detachment from the object of the concentration. Finally, it is like looking into emptiness and listening to stillness; and sense of bodily feelings and position are lost. Feeling of the personality disappears, and everything dissolves into light and then into clarity, as though the universe has never existed. Thus, Samadhi leads to emptiness. This first type of concentration should be done regularly at least once a day for 20-30 minutes.

The second type is a unifying concentration. Here, the observer unifies himself with the object of concentration. It is as though he has entered the object and feels himself to be the object on which he is concentrating. For example, if a person is concentrating on a wall, he forgets that he is a person and feels that he is this wall. The observer becomes the observed; the thinker becomes the thought. This is called Samayama. During the Samayama type of concentration, the feeling of "I" can be put not only into one object, but also into the whole universe. At that point the division between "I" and "not I" disappears. There is no "I" and "not I", everything is the same. Only Samayama on the whole universe is the right type of concentration leading to realization because Samayama on less than the whole consciousness supports duality by splitting the universe into "I" and "not I."

It is recommended to do Samayama on rays of the rising and setting sun. Wherever the sun rays go, we are also there with our attitude of wishing happiness and enlightenment to the whole universe.

We can begin to do Samayama at any object. When we become proficient at it, we can spread it at the whole universe. Later we do not do it at an object, just at the whole universe. When

Samayama at the whole universe is done often enough and long enough, it leads to the unity of consciousness.

Concentration without an object can be done directly or indirectly. A direct concentration without an object is done with open eyes, not looking at anything particular, and not paying attention to any objects, feelings or thoughts. Concentration should not be forceful, rather gentle, but firm, even flowing and stable like staring at nothing without thoughts. Body and perceptions must be relaxed. There should be detachment and indifference to the entire content of consciousness. We stay unattached and undistracted, not wanting anything, not rejecting anything, and not expecting anything; just resting and maintaining keen attention.

The fastest way to learn concentration without an object is to wake up at three o'clock in the morning and sit in the bed in a lotus position with open eyes for about fifteen to twenty minutes. During this meditation we do not do anything, just sit and rest. It is important to sit and to have open eyes; otherwise instead of concentration, the mind becomes dull and we fall asleep.

Indirectly, concentration without an object can be done by concentrating on a point of light in front of oneself or above one's head until the universe and space disappears. Then, one lets go of that point and continues in concentration.

When, during the concentration without an object, everything disappears - including oneself and the universe - then the concentrator becomes spaceless emptiness. After the emptiness, the realization of unity of consciousness appears by itself. Emptiness can be preceded by various experiences, pleasant or unpleasant - for example, by visions of gods or of terrifying figures called guardians of threshold, by fear, unpleasant thoughts, strong sounds, intense light, etc. When these come, it is necessary to remember that they are only imaginations and they cannot be harmful. We must not mind them. We should ignore them and not be afraid of them, nor repel them, but continue in concentration.

If the experiences are pleasant, we should not be attracted to them or wish for them.

Before sleep, we can try concentration on a point of light in the center of the chest, or on a point between the eyebrows. It would be still better just to keep a pure attention three feet above the knees.

When the concentration becomes exhausting, we should alternate concentration with relaxation. The best way is to begin with concentration, and end with relaxation. Before or when tired during meditation, we can do simple breathing exercises consisting of hyperventilation. For a few minutes, we breath fast and deep. We try to exhale as much air from the lungs as possible and stay relaxed during this. An increased intake of oxygen to our brain sharpens attention and restores concentration.

CONTROLLING THE MIND

Control of mind is necessary to self-knowledge and correct behavior because thoughts are the causes of deeds. However, it is not the final method to attain realization because during control of mind, consciousness is divided into the controller, the controlling, and the controlled.

When we try to suppress thoughts before they arise, this effort increases the amount of thoughts in consciousness. If we persevere and increase the willpower, we learn how to cut off thoughts before they arise. At first we are more tense than usual, but later we learn how to perceive directly without thoughts, how to comprehend the situations without accompanying words, and how to understand concepts and situations without formulating them into words. This requires constant attention. When controlling the mind becomes a habit, then a clear state of relaxation with little or no thought appears when one is resting.

The next step is resting relaxed in a clear mind without thoughts, movement, or wanting.

MANTRA

Mantra is a syllable, word, or sentence repeated rhythmically and is an effective method for calming and immobilizing the mind. Mantra has to be repeated quickly in a relaxed way, so that no other thoughts jump into the mind - or if they do, so that mantra will replace them. The faster we say the mantra the better. The purpose of mantra is to make the mind non-moving and firm.

Mantra can have a meaning, and then has an autosuggestive effect. Mantra also can be a syllable without any meaning. The best of the autosuggestive mantras are CALM, QUIET, REST, or PEACE.

While saying mantras, we sit without any movement. An advantage is to take a rosary (beads) in our hands and count the number of mantras. The association of rosary with mantra, after some time, causes the mind to calm faster. To become effective, the mantra has to be repeated at least 444,000 times. Full effectiveness comes after 10,000,000 repetitions. If possible, at the beginning mantra should be said aloud three or four times and then repeated in the mind silently, rhythmically, quickly, easily and automatically with steady attention, and without any purpose or effort. When mantra stops by itself and the mind does not move, it is not necessary to develop an effort to continue by force. Only when a thought comes, we need to replace it with mantra - this means, to again repeat the mantra as before. Between every two mantras, there is a clear, immobile, firm, resting consciousness.

During the recitation of certain mantras, it is recommended to create visions, most often of one's guru, personal god, or mandala (mandala is a symbol of universe). The vision should be created and be present during the entire recitation of mantra. When the recitation is finished, the whole vision should be dissolved into light, and the light should be shrunk and concentrated into one point. Then, we should let go of that point of light and continue concentration without an object, not minding any experiences eventually presenting themselves.

BREATHING

There are many ways to use breathing for meditation. One of the best proven and most recommended method is counting the number of breaths for 24 hours up to 23,000 breaths without interruption. Also, we can count them up to ten inhalations at a time, then start over again from one to ten, and use beads to register the 23,000 count.

The most simple way of meditation on breath is the following one. We fix our attention on our regular breathing without any counting. We follow the air at the site of nostrils. But mainly we follow the immobile pauses and quietude between the inspiration and expiration and, also, between the expiration and inspiration. When we become aware of immobility and tranquil unchangeability, we keep that awareness constantly during the breathing movements, relax into it, and rest in it. We consciously stay in this immobility as long as possible, even when we work, eat, go to bathroom, or lay down in bed to sleep. We have to be content with that immobility, quietude, relaxation, and rest. We cannot do more than be aware of it and surrender to it. This immobility and rest will gradually deepen by itself.

RECAPITULATION

While in bed before sleep and with closed eyes, we recall all important happenings of the past day backwards, beginning with this evening and ending with this morning. We become aware of all of the right deeds we have done and decide to continue them. In the same way, we become aware of all our mistakes and decide to get rid of them. We have to see our person objectively as though it were somebody else and we were just an indifferent observer criticizing his or her motivations and deeds. Then, we imagine how ideally we will act during our sleep - dreams have to be under our control, too - and during the next day. Our motivation has to be unselfish and altruistic.

Similarly, when awakening in the morning, before we get up from bed, we have to recall all our dreams backwards, beginning with the last one and ending with the first one. We regret all mistakes done in our dreams and decide not to repeat them. In the same way we recall all our right actions and motivations in our dreams and decide to continue them. Then, once more, we imagine how ideally we will behave during the coming day. During this, again, we are looking at our person in a detached, impersonal way as though it were somebody else and not us. In this way we become an impersonal observer of our ego. This will help to remove the division between us and the universe. We will feel that we are, also, the other persons and objects and that their being and substance are us, and we will treat them as ourselves.

CONTROLLING THE DREAMS

That which is aware of dreams and creates them is the ultimate immortal reality and substance of everything; it is the same as during the waking state. We have to be aware of it constantly, not only during the waking but also during the dreaming state.

Before we can control dreams we must become aware that we are dreaming and the dream is our creation. This can be accomplished by several means.

First, before sleep, we make and maintain a firm decision that during sleep we will be aware that we are dreaming and that dreams are only our imaginations. Second, while awake, we constantly are aware that the waking state is like a dream and that it is just an imagination. Third, every morning, we try to recall all of the dreams of the past night, and it is even more helpful if we write them down. If this does not work, let us find what in our dreams is unrealistic and absurd. Then before sleep let us make a firm decision that anytime we dream of this again, we will become aware in our dream that it is just an unrealistic dream and not a waking state. For example, if we dream about flying just by flapping our arms, we immediatelly become aware that this cannot be reality but is just a dream. Also, it is helpful to rest on the right side, or to have more pillows under the head. Then, if we still do not achieve the desired result, it is recommended to imagine a red syllable OM in the throat and repeat it silently as a mantra when falling asleep. Or we can use electronic devices to help us become aware that we are dreaming.

After we learn to be aware during the dream that it is just a dream, the next step involved in controlling the dreams will be an easy one. We will be able to direct the dreams, to create them, and to use them for meditations and improvement of our character. It will bring us many other advantages if we avoid using dreams for selfish purposes. For example, creative abilities and possibilities to solve problems that are unsolvable in a waking state can come during dreams.

The difference between a waking state and a dream will gradually become less and less. Some dreams can become more real than the waking state. The personality of the waking state will become as unreal as the personality of a dream. The feeling of reality will be transferred to a common denominator of the waking and dreaming state, that is - to the intelligent, brilliant, formless, eternal consciousness.

SLEEP

Sleep without dreams is similar to the realization of clear, empty consciousness but has the disadvantage of not being remembered. During sleep, there are no imaginations, no feeling of "I," no memory. However, this does not mean that our consciousness, our real being, does not exist during sleep. We simply do not remember it because in sleep nothing is happening. There is no attention, memory, time, or space. However, the formless consciousness is still there, and it is possible for us to remember it with the help of the following meditation.

While falling asleep, we are gradually losing awareness of the legs, trunk, neck, and, finally, of the head. Then, for a very short moment, we find ourselves in a transitional state of empty consciousness, and then we loose awareness in the deep sleep.

This transitional state of clear consciousness without any form can be grasped while falling asleep and can be consciously maintained uninterrupted during deep sleep for the entire night and, also, remembered. The easiest way of doing this is during falling asleep to imagine clear, pure, empty consciousness as a brilliant light of attention about three feet above our knees. We have to do this in an easy, relaxed manner without thoughts. It is recommended that we go to bed one hour earlier then usual. Although we will not be able to prevent loss of "I" and time, we will not lose awareness during the sleep and will remember that state after awakening. There will be no dreams, and we will be fully rested and recovered. It will seem to us that only a split of a second has elapsed between falling asleep and awakening; although, indeed, we have slept a full seven to eight hours.

We should not get discouraged if we do this many times and do not succeed. When we learn to maintain that state during sleep, this clear, impersonal, timeless state will gradually spread to our waking state.

RECOLLECTION

"Show me the face you had before your parents were born!" This was the task given by a Zen master Honrai No Memmoku to his student. To recollect this was a task using memory. Thinking could not solve the task. When the student fulfilled the task, he got realization.

We have to recollect gradually, day by day, all of our childhood memories until we get to the point in time when we had not yet felt like a person, this means not felt like an "I." We have to turn the flow of time backwards. By doing this we find that the existence of time is illusory; time is our imagination; and present experiences are as illusory as the past ones. Only the presence itself is real, and nobody can get behind it or ahead of it. All thoughts are based on the present memory and are active only in the present presence. We are this presence that has no face or form, was never born, will never die, and is eternal.

PRESENT PRESENCE

Everything exists only "here," in consciousness, inside of it; nothing can exist "there," outside of consciousness. This is because all space is only in consciousness and there is no space outside of consciousness for any objects. Nobody can get beyond "here," beyond the presence.

Similarly, everything exists only in the "now" and nothing can exist in the past or the future. We can become aware of the past or future only as a thought or an imagination existing exclusively just in the "here and now," in the present presence.

We can become aware of the present presence directly and immediately here and now. The whole universe, including the body, feelings, emotions, and thoughts, constantly is changing in the present presence, but the present presence remains the same -

unchangeable, firm, immobile, and real. It has no beginning and no end. Everything is impermanent and transitory; only the present presence itself is eternal. It is tranquil, silent, content, simple, and not made of anything or by anything. Present presence is the basis of everything and creates everything. We also call it truth, consciousness, etc.

If it is difficult to immediately grasp the present presence and be constantly aware of it, then we can first imagine a personified god or a guru and feel his presence. When the feeling of presence of god or guru intensifies and solidifies so that we feel it permanently day and night, then we have to keep just that living, intelligent presence itself and let go of the image of god or guru because they are just imaginations - forms of the formless. Present presence then will become a firm formless reality.

The next step is to see the difference between that reality and that which is unreal. This should be done by seeing or perceiving - not by thinking. The sight has to be directed at the perception of reality and at attentively watching the difference or identity of the reality and the perceived states of consciousness.

It is not sufficient to make theoretical conclusions about the present presence and about the unity of consciousness, i.e., to create concepts about them. One has to perceive the unity directly by senses, feel it, and be it.

THE SERPENT'S PATH

Between every two thoughts, there is a gap where consciousness is without manifestation, without form. Similarly, as a serpent slides into a gap between two rocks, also, our attention has to slide between two thoughts into consciousness without form.

While the mind is slowed down during meditation or relaxation, it is easier to grasp that formless element between two thoughts or imaginations. This element is a source of thoughts, stuff from which the thoughts are formed and into which they dissolve. Mind, at the time of slowing down, moves like a cog-wheel with interruptions, jumping from one thought to another similar thought; or like bullets from a semi-automatic gun, triggered one after another by attention. Usually when the mind is not slowed down, thoughts go fast, like bullets from an automatic gun, and it is difficult to catch the gap between them.

Thoughts should not be suppressed or removed; rather we should see how they arise and disappear. It is like seeing formless emptiness, hearing stillness, and feeling the presence of a formless, immobile substance from which the thoughts are forming and into which they are disappearing. All things seem to be just a surface of that unfathomable substance.

When we get a glimpse of the presence of unmanifested consciousness, we should keep our attention focused on it without movement and should ignore any thoughts, feelings, or perceptions; but we should not suppress them. Then, the feeling of duality and personality disappears and the contradiction between ego and objects ceases. Clear, formless, timeless being becomes apparent.

WALL

When we look at an empty wall in front of us, we feel that the wall is immobile, non-changing, firm, and hard. However, we know very well that after some time this wall will fall apart and that the particles of which it is made are moving and changing unceasingly.

We have to be aware that the hardness and firmness does not belong to the wall, but it is the substance of our consciousness that is hard, firm, unchangeable, and immobile. Let us constantly hold onto that immobility and unchangeability and know that it is our consciousness, our substance, our most basic being. In such a way, we can meditate not only on a wall, but also on any non-moving, firm, and hard object - for example, a rock, mountain, earth, diamond, etc.

All things in the universe will fall apart; but the basic being - pure consciousness itself - will never fall apart, will not change, and will stay forever the same because it is the simplest, uncomposed substance of everything. An infinite number of universes arose, fell apart, perished, and will arise, fall apart and again perish. Only that hardest and firmest substance always remains as a stable, unchanging, timeless, and eternal being.

The expression "diamond being" indicates the hardest and firmest state. The state of "diamond being" is identical with the feeling most people have about their own immortality. They feel they will never die, even when they see others around them dying. This feeling is an indication - an intuition - of what they really are; and it is correct concerning their basic being, but it is not correct concerning their egos and personalities. This mixed, erroneous feeling is similar to an impure, dirty diamond. A dirty diamond has very little value. But if it is without impurities, it is precious.

FOOD

Everything is made of the substance of consciousness, including food and drink. Whenever we eat or drink, we are taking this substance of consciousness into the body and changing it to the body.

When we eat and drink, we have to be aware that food and drink is, in reality, made of the substance of sacred consciousness and that this substance is changing into our body. Food and body are of the same nature as consciousness. Food and body are similar objects and, indeed, they are the same sacred being.

We have to look at food and body from a higher viewpoint, as a divine, sacred means enabling us to attain realization. We should not feed ourselves just to remove hunger but also to make the body strong and healthy so it will be a carrier of realization. Being strong, healthy and living long, we can help more people to realization and liberate them from unnecessary suffering.

THE NON-MOVING

In the whole universe, nothing is immobile. Everything is moving and changing incessantly. Only the substance of consciousness, its basis, is not changing and remains firm, stable, and immobile.

Whatever we are perceiving as immobile, firm, and non-changing - whether it be a desk, wall, rock, mountain, a piece of iron, earth under our feet, space, etc. - let us fix our attention on it and keep that firm, immobile feeling. Let us not deceive ourselves that whatever induced the feeling of immobility is immobile; but let us be aware that this immobility belongs to our consciousness and not to the object.

The immobile, non-moving and unchangeable is omnipresent. Without it we are not able to become aware of any movement or change. This is the same as in the theory of relativity: when two trains are moving close to each other at the same speed, the travelers cannot see that they are moving. Only if one of the trains is not moving or is moving at a different speed, can they see the movement of the other train.

Until now, our attention - for practical purposes of life - has been directed only at the moving and has been neglecting the non-moving. Therefore from now on, we should pay attention mainly to the non-moving, firm and non-changing - to that which is always the same. At the same time, however, we should not refuse to be passively aware of any movements or changes of anything in our consciousness.

When we already see the non-moving, we should focus on both the moving and the non-moving at the same time, and we should find out how the two differ. This should be done by seeing, not by thinking. Then we should look at both of them again and try to see how the non-moving becomes the moving and how the moving becomes the non-moving. Neither the first nor the second one should be done by intellectual analysis. They should be done by direct sight perception. Intellectually, we already have learned from previous sections that both the non-moving and the moving are manifestations of consciousness and are a unity. Now, we need to perceive this directly and immediately without any concepts.

STILLNESS

After listening to sounds attentively with concentration and without thoughts, we also can hear stillness as a contrast to the sounds. We should not imagine stillness, but hear it in the same way and as clearly as we hear sounds. We should not remove the sounds, nor should we plug our ears, but we should perceive everything, i.e. sounds and stillness. We do not think about the stillness; we just hear it. It takes only time and increased attention in the direction of stillness to hear it. Rock-and-roll and similar noisy music induces stillness easier than low sounding music because it creates a bigger contrast to stillness. However, let us not damage our ears by strong, noisy music. When we have briefly caught stillness several times, then we can become aware of that stillness without a noise.

Stillness is a stable, unchanging, quiet, and eternal existence. It is firm, immobile and all sounds are in it and from it. Let us listen to stillness as long as possible. When somebody is an auditory type, this meditation on stillness is more effective than visual ones. Everything is happening in that stillness. Every sound and form are made of this total stillness.

MEDITATION WHILE DRIVING AN AUTOMOBILE

Sometimes, when we are standing on a bridge and looking down at the flowing water, it seems to us that the water is still and the bridge is moving up the river. Similarly sometimes when we are driving a car, especially at night on an empty highway, it seems that we are immobile and the road and country is running to us. This illusion is helping us remove the illusion about the split between us and the rest of the world. It is like pulling a thorn from our foot with the help of another thorn.

Let us spread that illusion of the running road and country to the whole consciousness and let us perceive everything in the entire consciousness - including our body - as moving and changing. The whole universe with our body and the car is changing, only our consciousness itself is non-moving, stable, firm, and unchanging. We have to feel that we are that which is non-moving, and we should identify ourselves with the non-changing and with that tranquility of the consciousness that is passively aware of everything. We, also, should try to feel and be this non-moving when we stop and get out of the car.

The advantage of this meditation is that we unconditionally must stay alert and preserve a keen attention and concentration because we are driving a car. Also, in this way, we learn to meditate during an activity, not only during rest.

ATTENTION

The flow of attention is usually directed from consciousness to objects and feeling of "I." The task is to stop that flow of attention, let go of all awareness of the personality and the universe, maintain only pure attention without any objects, and rest. The attention should be clear, pure, and empty of space and objects to which it could cling. This is similar to a concentration without an object.

If possible, such meditation should be done suddenly, at once, and totally, without any preparatory steps whenever we have a free moment. Looking at nothing, we have to rest with a stopped memory as though the whole universe has never existed, as though we were awakened from a dream about our person and the universe.

If it is difficult to do this mental exercise at once, we can do it step by step. First, let us look at the objects in front of us. Then, we stop noticing them as though they were made of a transparent glass and as if we were looking at the emptiness behind them. During this, we keep our eyes entirely open.

Then, we look at our body in a similar way as though it does not belong to us and as if it were separate from us. We look through our body without any interest as though through a window glass at empty space.

We do not pay any attention to thoughts and feelings. We keep only clear attention, not directed to anything. We ignore all awareness of anything; and we rest inactive, keeping the pure attention itself as long we can.

When the attention becomes stable, firm, and unchanging, we should not try to get beyond that unchanging because we ourselves are that. We relax into it, surrender to it, and rest in it like in an unconquerable fortress. We return back to this state as often as possible. This becomes a total rest and relaxation for our worried and tired mind.

Another way of maintaining pure attention is with the help of reverie. We follow a chain of thoughts or imaginations with our eyes open, looking in front of us, a little upwards. When we finish that chain of thoughts or imaginations we do not start a new chain, but rest relaxed, with our eyes open and with keen attention fixed in the same way as before, but this time without any imaginations and thoughts. For example, we can try to figure out - just in our mind, without any paper and pen - the total of 423 times 127. When we finish that task, we do not start any new thought, imagination or task. For as long as we can, we relax, rest, and keep our attention keen in the same way as it was during the task.

Yet another way of maintaining pure attention is by trying to solve an unsolvable task; for example, imagine a circle with four 30 degrees angles; or a barren woman's child; or how to get a duck out of a narrow necked glass bottle alive without breaking the bottle; or a classical Zen koan: to hear the sound of one hand clapping. After trying hard and long - day and night - to solve such a task, we have no other possibility but to relax and keep our attention as sharp and fixed as during our attempts to solve the task. Success can come only after a real and long effort.

DEATH

Meditation on death is one of the most effective means to attain realization. During death, nobody and nothing can help us except realization. Before our death, only realization can supply us with a certainty of what will happen to us when our body will have died.

During the death of body and personality of each living being, a realization happens automatically. Even though it is too late to live that realization, it helps remove the fear of the unknown which can come during a slow death.

Imagine that we have died and nothing exists any more - no body, no universe, no personality, no space, and no time. There is only eternal rest, absolute spaceless emptiness, and tranquility. Nothing is moving, and nothing is happening. Existence and non-existence are the same, and nothing matters. It is the end of everything, and there is no goal, no purpose, no meaning, and nothing to achieve. There is no memory; it is as though the whole universe, including our person, never existed. There is an absolute peace, relaxation, and rest. There is no realization, just an absolute emptiness and rest. There is nothing to do or to want. Indeed, it is impossible to do or to want anything anymore.

When we die psychologically, there is nothing to be afraid of any more. The worst that can happen has already happened to us. Thus, to die psychologically before we die physically is an advantage. Beginning with the psychological death, our life will be without fear, wanting, existential anxieties, and worries; and it will be peaceful and calm. It will be just a play. No fear of death will be felt because to die twice is impossible.

That which is manifested in us is impermanent and is dying and being reborn constantly, from moment to moment. That which is unmanifested in us is eternal and cannot die under any circumstances. Whether we know it or not, we are always the unmanifested and eternal, and we have no reason to be afraid of anything or to want anything more.

LOOKING INTO THE MIND

Mind is that which creates everything - not only thoughts, but also imaginations, wanting, feelings, emotions, perceptions (objects), space, and time. Mind is like a shiny crystal ball in which there is entire space, the universe of which we are conscious at the given moment - including our body and feeling of "I" - and in which everything is incessantly changing from one thing into another. Mind is the active, manifested part of consciousness. While the mind is actively imagining things, consciousness is passively aware of the manifestations of mind. Mind is personal. Consciousness is universal and impersonal. Empty mind or mind itself is the concept closest to consciousness; and like consciousness it is regarded as a sacred symbol of the basic reality and ultimate truth.

Let us find the place where we create our thoughts and forget what we were told at school - that this place is in the brain. Let us try to see, not to think, where that place is. Usually, it is above the head a little to the front. Emotions are usually felt in the chest. We should observe how thoughts arise and how they disappear. Let us find out of what material they are made. When we watch thoughts with a keen interest, they slow down and then they stop arising. Even if a thought starts to arise, it is like a small cloud of steam that dissolves before assuming a definite shape.

To want something, to not want something, to cling to something, to try to get rid of something, hope, and hopelessness are also thoughts. Similarly, as we sit on the bank of a river, just watching it and not interfering or influencing its flow, we should be looking at the thoughts and emotions passively but attentively, not interfering with them. It does not matter if they are good or bad, we must not try to change or influence thoughts in any way.

Now, we pay attention to the nature of mind itself. We try to see what kind of shape , color or sound it has and of what it is made. While doing so, we must not think or make concepts about it, but try to perceive it (see, hear or feel it) immediately and directly. Our attention should be keen, one-pointed, clear, and steady. If our attention deviates, we bring it back without any feeling of guilt, failure, or disappointment. When dull or tired, we do not force ourselves to overcome the fatigue. We rest a while, then try again to fix our attention on the substance of the mind - on the stuff of which it is made. When we come to the empty space, we have to know that also space is an imagination. The basis of mind has no space and is without center or periphery - clear, silent, eternal, alive, and intelligent.

As often as possible, we look into our mind and passively watch the changes within it without intervening with its processes. We have to look at the mind objectively as though it were somebody else's mind and see how it is active by itself - how everything in it is changing, moving, breaking, and jumping over from moment to moment. Only the immobile glare and clarity of attention in the background remain the same. This clear, pure immobile attention is the consciousness itself.

We should always remember that whatever appears in the mind, including light, clarity, etc. is just a concept. Everything is just an unreal imagination.

We have to live everything that is coming to our consciousness the way it comes, with an uninterrupted attention and without forgetting oneself in thoughts.

RELAXATION

During relaxation, we have to be sitting or half-sitting comfortably in the chair, on the floor, on the bed, etc. We cannot lay down, because we will fall asleep. A common, dull sleep interferes with meditation. The best way is to sit comfortably with the spine straight up and with hands in the lap or on the thighs.

First, we should relax the muscles of the right hand (if left-handed, relax those of the left hand). If relaxation is not successful, then the muscles of the hand first have to be tensed and then relaxed. This way, we learn what relaxation of the muscles feels like.

Then, we become aware of all the feelings in the hand without wanting to change or interfere with them in any way. We let them be the way they are. We have to be aware of the presence of the hand - its existence, pressure of its weight, touch on the lap (thigh), flow of blood, pulsation of vessels, warmth, tension, involuntary movements, shape, position in space, etc. We have to be aware of every finger separately, palm, back of the hand, forearm, arm, etc. Also, we should have awareness of eventual tingling, tickling, itching, restlessness, and all other feelings that occur in the hand. In this way, the hand will relax by itself more and more until it is totally loose and flabby. We have to put all of our attention and awareness into this.

Then we do the same with the left hand and gradually with the left leg, then the right leg. After the extremities, we do this with the entire body, from bottom to top: the lower part of trunk, abdomen, chest, neck, jaws and head. While at the chest, we should not forget to become aware of the breathing movements, heart beating, and then of air flowing through the mouth and nose.

After several sessions, the gradual relaxation is easy and fast. Then we do not need to relax the body gradually. In fact, we can relax the entire body at once, right from the beginning. We do this in such a way as to become aware only of the strongest feeling in the body. We do not try to remove that strongest feeling or change it. We leave it the way it is. We just watch it passively and see how it changes. As soon as any other bodily feeling becomes stronger, we shift our attention to that stronger feeling. The feelings will be changing and, finally, they disappear. When we do not have any feelings or when they are weaker than breathing movements, then we watch the breathing. While watching this, we become aware not only of breathing movements but, also, of the immobile intervals between breathing in and out and between breathing out and in. We should not try to control, direct or, change anything. Trying, or effort, is a tension and interferes with relaxation. Let everything be as it is. We just rest. If the breathing or the heartbeat slows down, we leave it that way. We do not consider it a mistake or a harmful condition.

We take the same attitude toward thoughts. We do not get attached to them and do not control, direct, or follow them. Do not forget, that giving to ourselves advices as to what to do with thoughts are also toughts. We are indifferent to them and detached from them. We just look at them passively and let them go wherever they want. We stay relaxed and rest. Every effort and wanting to do something is a tension, a disturbance from relaxation, and is an obstacle. Quietude, stillness, immobility, and rest do not require any effort or any doing. We let go of everything, relax passively, and surrender to tranquility. This way, the whole body and mind will become totally immobile and tranquil.

QUIETUDE

We constantly and silently repeat a mantra: "QUIET" or "CALM." Or we can use a mantra that has no meaning. We do this not only when we sit in a meditative position, but also while we are active during the entire day. When we become aware of any immobile quietude or tranquility, we keep the awareness of it and relax into it. We rest in it as in our real, true home. When the quietude deepens, it becomes an absolute, stable, unchangeable presence that has no reason, cause, or purpose. This presence exists from eternity to eternity, is always the same - clear, silent, empty, permeates everything, and is an immobile basis of everything that moves and changes. Everything exists only in this presence, and everything comes from it. This is the ultimate, sacred, intelligent being that is the source and basis of the universe.

When we get up from such meditation, we do not finish it abruptly but we transit to our activity slowly and keep the quietude and contentment of meditation constantly, without any reason, during the whole day. That quietude can be accompanied by a happy, blissful, warm feeling in the heart. We do not suppress or remove this feeling, but we do not cling to it. If it is present, that is good; if it is not present, that is also good. We stay in the absolute quietude, stillness, and emptiness; we relax into it, and rest in it during our activities. We are content with it, surrender to it, and identify with it because, in reality, it is our quiet, pure, empty consciousness - and we are this consciousness.

PASSIVE AWARENESS

Quiet consciousness, without imaginations, is the unmanifested consciousness. Consciousness can come to the unmanifested state by a passive observation of mind.

Let us make a free time for meditation, at least after waking up in the morning. We sit or half-sit in a comfortable immobile position with open or half-open eyes. We stare in front of us as though into empty space. Let our thoughts arise, last, and cease in the way they want. We just rest and keep the mind quiet and content, without wanting or rejecting anything. We do not control, direct, or judge the thoughts - be they good or bad. We do not try to improve, change, influence or shape them even if they are bad. However, we do not get under their influence and do not unfold them or follow them. We are aware that they are arising and ceasing but we are indifferent and passive to them, and let them go wherever they want. We just look at them objectively with indifference, detachment, and without interest. This is the best way to learn how our mind works.

We leave everything in the whole consciousness the way it is and do not interfere with anything. We look at everything as at impermanent, transitory imaginations. Everything is an unreal imagination - this includes the body, emotions, feelings - including the feeling of "I" and personality - thoughts, endeavors, wanting, wishing, objects, universe, emptiness, fullness, etc. We are aware of the entire content of consciousness at once, not part by part. We should have a detached attitude to everything. Our slogan should be: quietude, relaxation, contentment, and rest from everything - just simply "to be" without doing anything. Realization is that what just is such as it is.

We have to look not only at the whole consciousness, but, also, at the emptiness around it; to listen not only to the sounds, but, also, to the stillness; to be aware not only of the movements, but, also, of the non-moving; to not suppress unpleasant or painful feelings, but to be aware of them with an indifferent and detached attitude. We look at our body with detachment as though it were not us but somebody else, as though it were just an object not belonging to us. Then, also, pain will be somewhere out there in the body and will affect us less.

If we cannot get rid of the judging and directing of what we should do and of how we should meditate, then, we have to observe that judging and directing. When a thought comes, we take an objective, detached, and indifferent look at it, as though we put it in front of us. We look the same way at every bodily feeling, emotion, reaction, and motivation as soon as they arise, from moment to moment. We should look at the entire consciousness, not just at its parts. This will induce quietude, emptiness, silence and stability.

When strong feelings or excitement come, we do not try to get rid of them. We leave them the way they are and use them for passive observation. When we have obsessive thoughts, we do not try to repel them; we should do just the opposite - purposely evoke them, think of them more, find of what material they are made, from where they originate, and to where they disappear. We do not try to overcome painful feelings, but to intensify them by paying even more attention to them and by finding of what material they are made. This way, all of the strong and painful feelings, emotions, and thoughts that seem to be obstacles will be changed into help in meditation.

This does not mean that we should do anything that comes to our mind. Thinking and doing are two different things. Our deeds must always be under our control, and our motivation always has to be unselfish. A thought which just passes through the consciousness, does not lead to action. If we get caught by a thought and unfold it, follow it, and continue it, then the thought will influence us and will cause us to act accordingly. Only then will the thought have some consequences (karma) for us.

If we try to become aware of pure, unmanifested consciousness, we create only an imagination, a concept about consciousness. Therefore, we just look at everything as at a transitory imagination, a concept, until we become quiet. Tranquility and detachment will come by themselves if we stay passive and uninvolved.

When we observe the content of our consciousness, we create an observer. However, keenly and calmly observed things disappear and dissolve by themselves. By an objective observation of the content of consciousness, everything gradually falls away like leaves from a tree in autumn or peels off like onion layers. Finally, when there is nothing to observe any more, the idea of the observer dissolves by itself and the consciousness itself comes to the quiet, unmanifested state. It does not observe anything anymore; it just rests and is. As soon as consciousness begins to observe anything again or becomes conscious of anything again, it is immediately out of this state. Just by seeing the observer as a thought, a concept, one can bring about the unmanifested state again.

The observer, observation, and the observed are imaginations. Also, the one who wants, the wanting, and the wanted are imaginations. Pure consciousness itself is not any of these.

We should not try to know anything, but just quietly, silently, passively, and with a keen attention and clear mind be aware of changes in the whole consciousness. We do not try to interfere with the observed processes and changes in consciousness. We have to live our consciousness in its natural state, the way it is. Then we will become peaceful and tranquil.

SURRENDER

We can get realization by doing any one of the before mentioned meditations (mental exercises). If insight into the truth does not come by having successfully accomplished the majority of these mental exercises, we have to assume a passive attitude and surrender to the highest intelligence and power of our own consciousness and leave everything up to its wisdom. This way, we remove the main obstacle which is our wanting, wishing, desiring and trying to secure something for ourselves; in short, we remove our own ego.

When the one who wants (i.e. ego) is strong, he covers that which is eternally present, real, and beyond time. At the moment when ego is helpless, unable to do anything, and surrenders itself, the veil of ego disappears and the timeless reality becomes apparent. At that moment, suffering disappears. When this happens, there is no wish. If the mind is not perfectly trained and guarded, the feeling of "I" comes back with a strong wish to maintain that reality for oneself, and this wish makes the ego strong again. This will again cover the real, eternal nature. The feeling of being a personality comes back again, and the ultimate reality seems to disappear. Sometimes, fear of losing realization also can sway us from it. It is a vicious circle. At that time, intellectual understanding of realization can be helpful. If we know that we always have been and will be that Ultimate Reality, then we know that we cannot lose it. It is possible to lose everything else, including our body, but not the reality because - as we are consciousness - we are that reality. We have just forgotten it. We are constantly hypnotized by our thoughts, concepts, perceptions and emotions that the world is real. Therefore, constant remembrance that the world is not real, and that our consciousness is the Ultimate Reality, is helpful.

We neither want nor try to get realization when we meditate. If we want realization that very wanting covers it. We just have to create conditions for it. We have to see that wanting and expecting something is a feeling, a concept; and we let go and do not touch that feeling. All we can do is be passively aware of changes in our consciousness without thinking, reflecting, judging, or concluding. Doing and effort are also concepts. All of these are only movements in our mind. We have to be like a small child who is just resting and neither knows nor remembers anything.

Let us rest without any movement in the tranquility of our consciousness while staying alert and mindful. Passive quietude, contentment, slowing down thinking, and stopping the mind will come by themselves if we rest mindful and detached long and often enough. When murky water in a pool settles down by itself, the water becomes clear and we can see the bottom. In a similar way, when the mind settles down by itself, we can see its basis. Interference with the pool will murky the water; interference with consciousness will agitate and veil it with its manifestations.

Everything is good the way it is. Let us be content with our fate and drop all the wantings. By surrendering ourselves to our destiny, we can become aware of that which is tranquil, immobile, formless, firm, empty, and real. Let us surrender to it, rest in it, and be in it always for it is our nature, our real being, us ourselves.

REST

Rest is done by sitting without any movement of the body. We do not pay attention to anything, do not look at anything, and keep the mindfulness and rest without any interest in anything. We let all the thoughts, feelings, and perceptions arise and vanish without any interest in them and without forming or influencing them. We just rest with the eyes open, not looking at anything in particular. We stay quiet, immobile, and do nothing. We let go of everything, relax, and take a rest from thoughts, problems, ourselves, and from the universe. We do not pay attention to anything, and we let the attention rest in itself. Concentration should be keen, steady, and flowing evenly. Empty consciousness cannot be cognized; we cannot become aware of it. We can only be it.

Even if consciousness has no shape, it is full of being; therefore, we rest in the absolute tranquility, stillness, relaxation, and immobility of pure being of consciousness. We drop everything, do not shape anything, and do not touch anything. We are relaxed, detached, and resting in the quietude, and stillness of clear, lucid consciousness. We are content with the tranquility, serenity, immobility, and rest. We let our worried and tired mind rest in the, clarity and immobility of our consciousness. There is no scattering of attention, no distraction, no sleepiness, no attachment to anything; no wanting, no rejecting, no expecting anything. Just resting relaxed and still.

Because all we can find is a creation of our own consciousness, there is nothing to search for. Even the knowledge of the ultimate truth and the feeling that we are everything is like looking at oneself in a mirror of one's own consciousness. When all we can find is consciousness, it is silly to look for anything. It is like trying to find our own eyes. What is then necessary, is the constant awareness that everything is a creation of our own consciousness. To remember this constantly from moment to moment is mindfulness. This will bring about stability, tranquility, and immobility. Then we really can relax, quiet down, be still, and rest.

We prolong and deepen that quietude, calmness, stillness, immobility, contentment, and rest. We relax and rest undistracted and detached. We surrender to that mysterious stillness and immobility, and we become it. We merge with it and get lost in it without any fear because we ourselves are it. We cannot do anything more. Everything else will come by itself. Any doing, wanting, or expecting whatsoever would interfere with the tranquility and stillness of that restful state.

* * *

The practical results of correct meditations are removal of selfishness, of fear of death, and of attachment to anything - including to one's own personality. There is freedom without limits, equilibrium of emotions, and stability of character.

HISTORICAL ADDENDUM

HINDU PHILOSOPHY

Vedas are the Indian sacred scriptures representing the Hindu philosophy. They already existed before the first millennium B.C.; although, most of them were written much later - some as late as the second century A.D. The origin of the Upanishads, the last part of Vedas, is usually placed in the beginning of the first millennium B.C.

The center of Vedic philosophy is the concept of Brahman, the Ultimate Principle, which manifests itself as the universe but has not exhausted its nature by its manifestation. It remains more than the universe. The doctrine of karma (law of cause and effect) and the doctrine of reincarnation are characteristic of the philosophy of the Upanishads.

The six classic systems or schools of Vedas are: Nyaya, Vaisesika, Samkhya, Mimamsa, Vedanta and Yoga. They represent a gradual interpretation of the Ultimate Reality. The seventh Hindu school, Kasmir Saivism, is the most logical. This idealistic monism is based on scriptures called Tantras and is partially independent of Vedas.

Nyaya, founded by Gotama (550 B.C.), is a system of logic that discusses the right knowledge and correctness of procedures. These are classified in sixteen chapters.

Vaisesika, founded by Kanada (third century B.C.), differentiates nine basic realities: earth, water, fire, air, ether, time, space, soul, and mind. It discusses their combinations and relations to the Ultimate Reality.

Samkhya was founded by Kapila (sixth century B.C.). It enumerates qualities of objects and establishes metaphysical categories (tattvas):

Purusa - impersonal soul, pure spirit.
Prakriti - primordial root, matter, nature.
Mahat - cosmic mind, will, intelligence.
Ahamkara - ego,("I").

Senses - sight, hearing, smell, taste, touch.

Manas - individual mind.

Organs - speech, hands, feet, excretory and reproductive organs.

Elements - ether, air, light, water, earth.

Yoga was founded by Patanjali in about the second century B.C.. It shows the means leading to the direct experience of objects and of the absolute. More about yoga is discussed later in a separate chapter.

Mimamsa offers rules for interpretation of Vedic texts, rituals, and rules for right action. Mimamsa was founded by Jaimini approximately between 600-200 B.C.

Vedanta, founded by Badarayana somewhere between 500 and 200 A.D., is an inquiry into the Ultimate Principle. Vedanta discusses the relationship between Brahman, matter, and world. It shows that absolute or ultimate reality underlines all objects and functions. The primal motion in nature is Brahman. Vedanta uses terms such as maya: false concept, illusion; avidya: ignorance; isvara: personified god; jivatma: individual soul; etc. and discusses the relationship between these concepts.

Three schools have developed from Vedanta:

Non-dualism (Advaita) was developed by Samkara (788-820 A.D.). This is monism: all is oneness, Brahman.

Qualified non-dualism (Visitadvaita) was developed by Ramanuja (1,027-1,147 A.D.). Brahman is real but, in the objective world, manifests itself as a duality.

Dualism (dvaita) was developed by Medhva (1,199-1,278 A.D.). Individual souls are separate from the Ultimate Principle and have an independent existence.

According to Vedanta, there are four prerequisites for the understanding of Brahman:

Right discrimination which results from proper study.

Right indifference which results from renunciation of the world.

Right conduct which consists of control of thoughts and senses, tolerance, endurance, faith, and mental and emotional equilibrium.

Desire to know the truth and to attain liberation.

Written in the Hindu philosophy is that a student passes through three stages: faith in the teaching of sages, understanding of the teaching, and realization of the truth. A remarkable idea of Hindu philosophy is that theories are not valid until they have been tested and proven in practical life. This idea is a basis of modern experimental science.

The seventh Hindu school, Kasmir Saivism, was founded by Vasugupta in the ninth century A.D. Consciousness (Parasamvit) is the Ultimate Principle and has two aspects: transcendental (Caitanya, Siva tattva) and immanent (Sakti tattva). Kasmir Saivism postulates ten more categories than Samkhya. Five categories higher than Purusa are: limited power, limited knowledge, desire, space, and time. Above them are five pure categories: all-powerfulness (Sadvidya), all-knowledge (Isvara), all-completeness (Sadasiva), all-pervasiveness (Sakti), and eternal existence (Siva). The highest category is Parasamvit (consciousness). Tantras deal with creation and destruction of the universe, worship, yoga, rituals, actions, and meditation. Knowledge alone is not enough. Final proof can be obtained only by personal spiritual experience; that is, by realization.

YOGA

The word yoga is derived from the sanskrit root "yujir" and means "union": the union of the individual soul (Jivatma) with the universal soul (Atman). Another possible root of the word yoga is "yuja" which means "to meditate."

Patanjali's Yogasutra defines yoga as: stopping of the functioning of the thinking principle (Yogas cittavrtti-nirodhah). The thinking principle (Citta) consists of mind (Manas), intelligence (Buddhi), and ego (Ahamkara). The thinker, or seer (Purusa), is our real self (Atman). Consciousness (Cit) is the essence of the self.

According to yoga, eight disciplines leading to enlightenment (realization), which should be practiced simultaneously, are:

Five abstentions from evil-doing (Yama) that means: not harming any living beings (Ahimsa), not stealing (Asteya), truthfulness (Satya), continence (Brahmacharya), not coveting (Asparigraha).

Five observances (Nyama): cleanliness (Saucha), contentment (Santocha), austerity (Tapa), study (Svadhyaya), devotion to god (Isvara pranidhana).

Posture (Asana).

Breath regulation (Pranayama).

Withdrawal of attention from sense-objects (Pratyahara).

Concentration (Dharana).

Meditation (Dhyana) - steady flow of the same thoughts and/or imaginations.

Samadhi - concentration with loss of personality feeling.

Obstacles to enlightenment include: ignorance (Avidya), attachment (Raga), aversion (Dvesa), and clinging to life (Adhinivesa). Minor hindrances to enlightenment are: sickness, languor, doubt, heedlessness, worldliness, erroneous perception, failure to attain concentration, or instability in the stage when attained. In order to overcome obstacles and hindrances it is recommended to imagine the opposite and to use any other conventional or unconventional means as long as they do not cause a permanent damage to physical or mental health.

Although yogis are considered to be ascetics, yoga forbids asceticism, self-mortification, and self-torturing. Bhagavadgita says:

> "The goal of yoga is not attained by the person who eats too much or who abstains from food, who oversleeps or

who keeps forcibly awake. The yoga which destroys pain is achieved by that person who eats and behaves as is proper and whose every action is led by reason and whose sleeping and waking are well regulated."

Nothing in yoga is considered supernatural. Miracles and strange phenomenas (such as visions, sounds, odors, and unusual feelings) are hindrances, or at best milestones, on the path. These occurrences should neither be wished for nor pushed away. They should simply be ignored and the exercise continued.

As to its practice, yoga is samadhi (Vyasa: Yogah samadhih). Samadhi has several degrees:

Samadhi with awareness of the object (samprajnata or savikalpa or sabija samadhi) with discrimination, reflection, bliss, and sense of being.

Objectless samadhi (asamprajnata or nirvikalpa or nirbija samadhi) is pure attention void of any object, ego feeling, memory, or thought.

Stabilized samadhi (turiya or sahaja samadhi) exists without interruption during waking, dreaming, and sleeping. This is the fourth state of consciousness.

Samayama is somewhat different from samadhi. Samayama is concentration where the concentrator loses the personality feeling and becomes the object of concentration.

Different kinds of yoga have different goals and employ different methods: Physical yoga teaches awareness, control, and relaxation of the body. It does not teach asceticism or harming of the body by unusual feats. Mental yoga supports tranquility of mind and calmness of emotions and promotes attention by mantras, rituals and other means. Here belongs philosophical yoga that promotes intuition and leads to direct insight into the substance of consciousness.

Classical texts usually recognize four basic kinds of yoga:

Hatha yoga - that means physical yoga.

Mantra yoga uses rhythmical repetition of sounds, words, or sentences.

Laya yoga, a yoga of mergence, uses unification by help of concentration. Here belongs Kundalini yoga (serpent power), Bhakti yoga (of love and devotion), Shabda yoga (meditation on sounds and stillness), etc.

Raja yoga uses creation and dissolution of visions, sounds, feelings, and other imaginations. Here belong Karma yoga (of duties and unselfishness), Jnana yoga (philosophical), and Siva yoga (of sleep, observation of mind, etc.).

All yogas are steps to an insight into the real nature of man and the universe.

HATHA YOGA

Hatha yoga, or physical yoga is the most familiar in countries to the west of India. At the very beginning, it is necessary to say that physical exercises and postures alone do not lead to realization. These only serve as preliminaries to mental and philosophical yogas. They help by teaching relaxation and awareness of the whole body.

Physical yoga has eight steps identical with the classical description in Patanjali's Yogasutra and is divided into two stages: outer and inner. The outer stage has abstinences, observances, postures, purifications, gestures (mudras and bhandas), and breathing exercises. The inner stage is represented by withdrawal of attention, concentration, meditation, and samadhi or samayama. (Note: Some physical purifications are dangerous and can cause health problems or death. Therefore, physical purifications should not be done without medical supervision.)

A posture means to remain motionless for a long period of time. Again, it is necessary to stress that some positions are dangerous; for example, a long headstand can cause brain damage.

Breathing exercises are done to sharpen attention. During all breathing exercises, the most important thing is to become aware of the immobile pauses between breathing in and out, and between breathing out and in.

Breathing exercises, done with a periodical contraction of perineum and anus, are called Mula-bandha. The exercises done with a periodical contraction of the abdomen are called Uddiana-bandha. If done with pressing the chin against the suprasternal fossa, they are called Yalandhara-bandha.

The most simple and most effective breathing exercise is paying attention to normal breathing without influencing it. To obtain the desired effect one must count the inhalations, up to 23,000 of them, without interruption of counting. Still, another simple breathing exercise is hyperventilation, i.e. deep and fast breathing done in a relaxed way.

In the most common yogic breathing exercise the inhalation lasts four seconds, holding of the breath for sixteen seconds, and the exhalation for eight seconds. When one does this type of breathing exercise excessively - too often, or prolonging the time, or too deeply - it can trigger emphysema or asthma, or can aggravate such conditions. Therefore, an excessive use of this exercise is not recommended.

Another breathing exercise used in Mantra and Tantra yoga is called Sukha (i.e. comfortable) pranayama. In a sitting position one closes the right nostril with right index finger and breathes out maximally through the left nostril. Then one inhales through the left nostril. After that, one closes the left nostril with the left index finger and exhales maximally. Then one inhales through the left nostril. Again, he starts with the right nostril and the right index finger. This breathing exercise is repeated at least three times, while saying mantras silently in one's mind; or just concentrating at the pauses between breaths without thoughts without saying mantras.

Fixation of sight (Trataka) is done by staring with unblinking eyes at a dot about six feet distant directly in front or on the floor. Turning the attention inside, away from the dot, after such fixation of sight is called Sambhavi-mudra.

Concentration on a perceptible form (thought, also, has a form) is called sarupa. Concentration without a form is called arupa.

Samadhi can be done by retaining awareness of the object. This is called samprajnata (savikalpa) samadhi. Samadhi without an object is called asamprajnata (nirvikalpa) samadhi.

Every kind of yoga can have a different name for the same type of concentration. All kinds of concentrations, visualizations and dissolutions of visualizations have the same purpose - to increase attention and comprehension.

MANTRA YOGA

In order to slow down the mind and finally to stop it, Mantra yoga uses rhythmical muttering of sentences (prayers), words, syllables, or sounds. They are mostly names of god(s), sacred syllables, or letters. These can be uttered aloud, muttered, whispered, thought, imagined, felt, or heard outside the body or inside the body at different organs and places. The most common requirement is a silent, mechanical, fast mental repetition of the same mantra at least twice a day before meals. Such a repetition is called Japa.

The most famous mantras are ÓM, ÁH, HÚM, RAM, YAM, KAM, HAM, AIM, SÓ-HAM, HRIM, KLIM, STRIM, HA, etc. The pronunciation of the above mantras is similar to Spanish or German pronunciation. The English transcript is difficult. Mantra is given to the student according to the tradition of a particular school, intuitively, or is matched to the student's personality or age.

The sixteen steps in Mantra yoga are devotion; purity; posture; observances of astrological signs; good conduct; concentration; search for divine areas within oneself; breathing exercises; gestures; ritual offering of water, fire, and fruit; ritual worship of deities by incense, flowers, honey, and cloth; repetition of mantra; meditation on the chosen deity or guru; unification of mantra with the universe; and unification of oneself with mantra (everything is mantra). The mantra should be repeated in the mind until the mind becomes saturated with the mantra and stops.

When the mind stops by itself, without any thoughts coming to it, one should not try to repeat the mantra by force. One has to rest in the immobility, firmness, emptiness, and silence. Then when a thought comes, one has to replace that thought again by the repetition of mantra in an easy, effortless way.

During an advanced meditation of Mantra yoga, one can find the source of mantra. Thus, by the help of mantra, one can find the source of all imaginations, thoughts, feelings, sounds, and rhythms, i.e. of the whole universe.

The student proceeds gradually from the spoken mantra to the thought of mantra; then to the feeling of mantra and, when the mind stops repeating it, to a stable undefined state. This state is a great silence (Paravak), immobility, firmness, quietude, and pure, simple being. Mantra and silence are a unity.

YANTRA YOGA

Yantra, or mandala, is a diagram or picture symbolizing the universe. This symbol has a calming effect on mind.

The root sound of mantra and root symbol of yantra are closely related to one another. For example, the letter A corresponds with a triangle, fire, red color, and activity. Because many symbols and pictures exist, the amount of different yantras is innumerble.

Combination of mantra repetition and visualization of yantra (mandala) is more effective when done together, rather than when done separately. Repetition of visualization of a yantra and dissolution of it lead to an undefined, formless, stable, immobile existence that is a firm reality, and is always present here and now. When one becomes aware of this reality, one has to surrender to it, rest within it without wanting or fearing, and identify with it. This reality is our basic being.

LAYA YOGA

Laya yoga merges the contradiction of "I" and not "I" in the consciousness. To make the opposites merge, Laya yoga uses concentration, gestures, imaginations, and meditations. The recommendation is to wake up after midnight and practice by listening to the inner sound (i.e. stillness) with eyes and mouth closed, ears plugged by fingers, and body in a lotus position facing north (Shanmuki-mudra). One can also use other gestures, positions, and meditations.

Laya yoga has the following parts: abstinences, observances, postures, gestures, breathing exercises, withdrawal of attention from outside objects, or concentration on Kundalini and Chakras (described in the next chapter). It also involves listening to the inner sound, meditating on light, merging with the sound or light, and, finally, finding the source of sound or light and identifying with it.

Listening to the inner sound is called Shabda yoga. Immobilized in Vishnavi-mudra, the yogi listens to the inner sound until he hears it and until the inner sound becomes stronger than the outer sounds. This begins with fine, subtle sounds like the humming of a bee, music of a flute, ringing of a bell, or beat of a small drum and ends with strong sounds such as the noise of the ocean, a big drum, or thunder. Then comes the strong silence and emptiness into which the yogi relaxes and merges.

During the meditation on light, one has to create a vision of light or immobile fire above one's head or in front of oneself. With the continuation of the vision, the light will become stronger, clearer, and purer. Then it has to be concentrated into one point. When the yogi continues in concentration keeping the mind immobile and letting go of that point of light, he becomes a clear, pure, timeless, spaceless consciousness which cannot be described because this is beyond form, time, and space.

KUNDALINI YOGA

According to yoga, Kundalini Sakti (The Serpent Power) is a potential energy located in the perineal region. It is coiled in three and half coils in the center called Muladhara Cakra.

Yoni mudra is the name of the technique used for the awakening of Kundalini Sakti and that can lead to liberation. Requirements for the use of this technique are absolute sexual abstention - both physical and mental - for at least three weeks prior to the technique, purification, courage, steadiness, endurance, subtlety, and imagination. One should be satisfied only with a direct experience. All the energy of the meditator must be sublimated into Kundalini.

One sits in a yogic position, with crossed legs touching the perineal region with the left heel (Siddhasana position). Eyes are closed, and ears are plugged by thumbs. In this posture, one does breathing exercises and chants the mantras HUM-HAM-SAH, imagines and concentrates on sexual lust, makes contractions of perineum, and imagines the Muladhara Cakra in his perineum. The awakening of Kundalini is accompanied by characteristic feelings, sounds, or visions. A sign of success is a feeling of pleasant, concentrated energy arising from perineum through the middle of the spine (Susumna) upwards to the head.

Having awakened Kundalini, the student forces it to pass through the seven centers in his spine which are called cakras. He does this by imagination of cakras, mantras, breathing exercises, and will. He leads Kundalini through the top of his head, above the head, and keeps it immobile one to two yards above the head. On its way upwards, Kundalini by itself may open special forces, feelings, sounds, and visions.

The first center is called Muladhara Cakra. Location: perineum. Form: four petal lotus. Color: yellow. Center of the lotus: triangular (triangle of knowledge, will and action). Kundalini shines there like a bright lightning energy coiled into three and half coils. Consistence: solid (earth). Function: cohesion, smell. Mantra: LAM. Deity: child Brahma. Manifested power (goddess): Sakini Devi.

The second center is Svadhistana Cakra. Location: base of the spinal column. Form: six petal lotus. Color: white. Center of the lotus: crescent moon. Consistence: liquid (water). Function: contraction, taste. Mantra: VAM. Deity: Visnu. Manifested power: Rakini Sakti.

The third center is Manipura Cakra. Location: in the spine at the level of navel. Form: ten petal lotus. Color: red. Center of the lotus: triangular. Consistence: energy (fire). Function: cleansing, sight. Mantra: RAM. Deity: Rudra. Manifested power: Lakini Devi.

The fourth center is Anahata Cakra. Location: spine at the level of heart. Form: twelve petal lotus. Color: pink. Center of the lotus: two triangles. Consistence: gaseous (air). Function: movement, touch. Mantra: YAM. Deity: Isa. Manifested power: Kakini Devi.

The sixth center is Ajna Cakra. Place: brain at the level of eyebrows. Form: two petal lotus. Color: snow white. Center: triangle in a circle. Consistence: primordial power (space). Function:

meditation, thinking. Mantra: OM. Deity: Atman. Manifested power: Hakini Sakti.

The seventh center is Sahasrara Cakra. Location: top of the head. Form: thousand petal lotus. Color: void (colorless clarity). Center: sun on the crescent moon. Consistence: formless, eternal consciousness. Function: unity, enlightenment. Mantra: HAM-SAH. Deity: Parama Siva. Manifested power: Sankhini Devi.

An abbreviated Tibetan version of Kundalini yoga is called Phowa. One imagines himself as being a realized goddess, a Red Vajra Yogini, and above her head a red Buddha sitting on a thousand petal lotus on a cushion of a crescent moon and sun. In her spine (i.e. spine of the meditator) is a blue Susumna (channel for energy). At the level of the heart is a green dot of energy. On it is a red syllable HRI equivalent to Kundalini and representing consciousness of the meditator. One repeats mantra HRI twenty-one times and then shouts out one syllable PHET while imagining the syllable HRI rising through Susumna above the head to the red Buddha. Then one unifies HRI with the red Buddha and keeps consciousness unified with the Buddha's mind. The sequence of this meditation has to be repeated as many times as necessary to achieve success. Every Phowa meditation should be finished by 111 longevity mantras OM-A-MARANYI-JIVANTI-YE-SO-HA. This type of meditation can be practiced only under a guidance of an experienced lama.

At the time of death of a person who has not attained realization, a special type of Phowa is done by a lama (Tibetan priest) experienced in Phowa at the bedside of the dying person. Tibetans believe that this way a lama can help a dying person attain realization.

BHAKTI YOGA

A Bhakti yogi has an intense love for his personal god. He loves all; he hates none (Vairatyaga).

Preparatory means for Bhakti yoga are observing commandments of his religion, love for his own personal god (Isvara), self-control, discrimination, charity, self-sacrificial work for others, purity, health, mental strength, truthfulness, sincerity, not coveting, not injuring anybody and anything, thinking only necessary thoughts, non-attachment, control of excessive joy and sorrow, and self-surrender to god.

A Bhakti yogi constantly repeats the name of his god, in the way a mantra is repeated. The nine steps in Bhakti yoga, as mentioned in Vishnu Purana, are listening to everything good spoken about god, singing praise to him, imagining him, worshiping his feet, worship by rituals, obeisance, becoming his slave, becoming his friend, and total self-surrender to god.

By seeing god in everybody and everything a Bhakti yogi tries to forget himself and gradually expands his love. He loves his wife and children more than himself. Next, more than himself, he loves his village, town or city; then his nation; his race; the whole of mankind; and all living creatures. Finally, he loves the whole world and the universe and its creator - god - more than himself. He is gradually giving up the less for the more. God is an universal love to him. Love becomes more than he, and he knows no fear. He gives all and requires nothing. He is not begging selfishly for his salvation. He loves god, not as servant loves his lord, but as a mother loves her child, or as a man loves his sweetheart. He forgets himself in his love. Love helps him feel identical with the object of his love, with god, and enables him to meditate constantly. Through every face and every object shines his beloved. He sees the divine principle in everything equally - in good as well as in bad. He sees that good and bad are relative concepts, dependent on the standpoint. Suffering is only lack of love and compassion for living beings and is just a result of selfishness and recklessness toward others. Love is creating and maintaining the universe.

Because love is a manifestation of mind and is not its basis, Bhakti yogi must get beyond love. The last step in Bhakti yoga is to find the source of love: that which is beyond the universe and beyond its creator, that from which the love arises and into which it dissolves. Finally, the Bhakti yogi will understand that his consciousness is the source of love, and that the universe and he himself are that source and the basis of everything.

ROYAL YOGA

Royal yoga is a yoga of imagination, concentration, will-power, mind control, and knowledge of the functioning of mind. Preparatory steps for Royal yoga are the same as for Hatha yoga.

The next step is creation of imaginations and dissolution of them. Meditation in Royal yoga, according to Yoga Sara Sangraha, has four degrees: visualization and dissolution of visions which are called Vitarka; creation and dissolution of thoughts which are called Vichara; creation and dissolution of joy which are called Ananda; and concentration without an object which is called Asmita.

The Royal yogi transcends his personality, time, space, and causality by dissolution of his imaginations, thoughts, feelings, person, and the universe (perceptions) with the help of concentration without an object. Constant observation of his mind without forgetting himself in its manifestations will bring him to a firm, immobile reality and the unity of consciousness.

SHIVA YOGA

Shiva yoga is described in Tantras. Shiva is an Indian god dissolving the universe. Shiva yoga practice is somewhat dissimilar to other yogas.

Having studied Vedanta, the yogi has no further need for thinking, contemplations, or imaginations. He meditates on three fundamental processes in nature called gunas. These three gunas are:

Raja guna: creation, evolution, action.

Sattva guna: lasting, intelligence, peace.

Tamas guna: descend, dissolution, dullness, passivity.

He does this in a hermitage - in a position called Svastika asana. He observes these processes in his consciousness without interfering with them - objectively, impartially, with indifference, and without any personal interest in them. He sees how all forms are formed from the formless principle of consciousness (Shiva), how they last only for a short present moment, and how they dissolve back into consciousness. The whole universe, including space, arises for a very short period of time. According to Shiva yoga, this period lasts for less than a billionth of time needed for a finger-snapping sound (modern physics states that a minimal period of time lasts for about 10^{-43} of a second). Then the universe disappears together with the space into emptiness for a timeless moment. Then, again, it appears - somewhat different - for the same long fraction of time. This is being constantly repeated. Such an appearance and disappearance compares to shooting bullets from a machine-gun. The universe is changing interruptedly and jerkingly, like a movement of a cogwheel; its basis (substance) remains immobile and non-changing. This can be seen when the attention becomes keen, and the mind slows down and eventually stops.

Because Shiva is also a god of sleep, the yogi practices meditation on sleep. This is described in the meditations section of this book.

PHILOSOPHICAL YOGA

The first and most important step in Philosophical yoga (Jnana yoga) is the desire to know the truth. Seeing the truth liberates a person from fear and unnecessary suffering. Philosophical yogi accepts nothing as true and sure without profound investigation. He makes the maximal possible use of his intellect before he transcends it. He does not throw it away right at the beginning as is done in religions and mysticism. He uses not only intellect and logic but also all his other abilities - especially objective observation, impersonal view, higher emotions (like love, compassion, good mindedness, etc.), concentration, endurance, charity, and other positive attitudes.

Study of science and philosophy brings him to the conclusion that something exists that is a basis, substance and source of the universe and, by this also, a source of himself. This substance is real, stable, non-changing, alive, intelligent, not influenced by space and time conditions, was never born and will never perish, and remains forever the same. It is beyond opposites and contradictions and is above all doubts. No theories or concepts can comprehend this substance. He will find that thinking or imagination cannot help him perceive or know this substance directly. Because this substance is his most basic being, all he can do is be it consciously and live it the way it is.

Intellectual realization is only a limited one. When Jnana yogi finds that nothing exists but consciousness and its manifestations, he sees the need to transcend his intellect by help of meditation exercises. It is not enough to have just an intellectual concept about the nature of the universe; it is also necessary to perceive correctly and feel properly the relationship between one's personality, the universe, and the Ultimate Truth, and to live that Truth such as It is.

Philosophical yoga is an experimental, not a theoretical, science. Philosophical yoga is based on experiments with one's own mind; therefore, meditation exercises are more important than intellectual analysis. Meditation, not thinking, facilitates realization. Love for truth does not mean love for ideas and concepts, but love for the intelligent basic reality and for the living substance of the universe of which we are created. Finally, all concepts must be put aside; otherwise, they will become obstacles to the realization of truth.

Practicing Philosophical yoga is like walking forwards and seeing the way far ahead. Practicing all other yogas is like walking backwards and seeing only that part of the way that has been traversed. The student of Philosophical yoga knows that everything is just an imagination of consciousness. He cannot miss the goal or mistake it for anything else, even without a teacher. He needs not to be afraid of anything, because everything can be understood, and everything can be turned into useful help on the way.

First, a yogi has to bring his thinking to the last concept, and then let go of that last concept. Thus he comes to a complete emptiness, without concepts, that resembles death. This way his thinking stops, and the truth reveals itself practically - not just theoretically by concepts. It is paradoxical, but true, that one can solve all the most important and most basic philosophical problems about oneself and the universe only when thoughts cease, the mind quiets down, becomes tranquil, and rests in quietude and eternity beyond time and space. Such realization of the ultimate truth brings certainty and contentment.

KARMA YOGA

Karma yoga is an ethical way of duties, work for the welfare and happiness of others, self-control, self-abandonment, self-sacrifice, selfless deeds, non-attachment, and objectivity. Karma yoga together with Philosophical yoga are like two wings of a bird carrying one fast to the goal. They complement each other.

Karma yogi does not act in order to have any personal profit from his activities. He only fulfills his duties and works for the welfare and realization of all beings in the whole universe. He forgets himself and sacrifices himself for others. He has rooted out every wish and desire for any fruit of his deeds. He accepts good and bad with equanimity. His mind is balanced. He puts aside his worries, anxieties, fears, resentments, and wishes. He does not care about his future because he believes in karma and that everything is in harmony with the mind. He lives just here and now in the present presence. He does what he considers to be right and is not concerned about the personal consequences and results of his deeds for himself. Therefore, he does not feel guilty about his past and does not worry about his future.

The Karma yogi lives in a mental and emotional equilibrium and peace. Because he does not mind himself, he does not want anything, does not avoid anything, and does not react negatively to anything. He does not avoid pain at any price. He just fulfills his duties, even if they are unpleasant to him. He is not afraid of death because his decision to sacrifice himself has made him psychologically dead anyhow. His ego has already died. Death is only a change of that which is temporary and must die anyhow sooner or later. He knows that his real being cannot change or die. He is not influenced by existential fears and does not refuse unfavorable consequences. Also, he does not wish for something that brings pleasurable feelings. He accepts everything that is coming, just as it is. He acts according to his conscience and cannot be bribed or influenced. He treats everybody, as he would himself, with love and patience.

GURU YOGA

Guru yoga is the fastest but often a difficult way to realization. The student gives up his own will and does only what his guru wants. He worships his guru, prays to him, meditates on him, takes care of him so that his guru has food, clothes, warm shelter (in hot countries a cool one), medicines - if needed - and serves him in other ways. Because a guru is the realization itself, the student identifies with his guru as his own ideal and goal during meditations. He should have a loving respect and unlimited trust in his guru. The student, also, has to respect and behave politely and decently toward the guru's posessions and family.

Only a person who has a permanent realization can be a guru. One or two experiences of realization do not qualify a person to become a guru. A guru must unconditionally have love, compassion, and a willingness to help his students achieve realization. He should know different ways and means to realization. He should be proficient in samayama so that he can transfer his realization to his students. He should be patient and forgiving. He must not be selfish or arrogant, nor should he teach the way to realization for money or a reward. He should not be a religious fanatic or a bigot, nor should he boast about his realization, knowledge, and abilities. He should not put importance on his reputation, position, glory, property, origin, tradition, lineage, and other worldly matters. If someone asks him if he has realization, he must not avoid the answer and must tell the truth. An evasive answer means that he does not have realization.

There are many examples of harsh treatment of a student by a qualified guru. For example, an Indian sage Tilopa ordered his student Naropa to jump from a high building. Naropa did so, broke his bones, and almost died; but later he attained realization. Milarepa had to build houses, then tear them down on the order of his Tibetan guru, Marpa. Peter was running away from Rome to escape persecution, but he had a vision of Christ who ordered him to go back. He returned and let himself be crucified. Gurdjiff ordered his student not to move from a deep ditch being flooded by water. The student obeyed and was drowning, but got realization during this incident. Gurdjiff pulled the half-drowned student out by the hairs on his head. Socrates obeyed his inner voice and let himself be poisoned. In all these examples, the students had to give up their personal decisions and their egos.

Realization depends more on a student than on a guru. If the guru is good and the student is good, the student will get realization. If the guru is not good and the student is good, the student still has a possibility of getting realization. If the guru is good and the student is not good, the student will not get realization. Of course, if both are bad, the student cannot get realization.

A famous Tibetan story relates it the following way. A Tibetan businessman went to India. His mother asked him to bring her a sacred object or relic on which she could meditate. The son forgot, but when he was close to his home, he recalled her request. He saw a dog's skull at the roadside. He pulled a tooth from the skull, polished it, and brought it to his mother, saying that it was a precious relic: Buddha's tooth. His mother meditated on the tooth and got realization. Since that time, there has been a proverb in Tibet: "Even a dog's tooth shines if it is meditated upon."

BUDDHISM

Buddha lived in the fifth century before Christ. He taught four noble truths:

All existence is suffering (or ends by suffering).

Suffering is caused by desire (wanting).

The extinction of desire leads to the extinction of suffering.

Extinction of suffering is an eightfold noble path: right view, right aspiration, right speech, right conduct, right livelihood, right endeavor, right mindfulness, and right concentration.

Because we are ignorant about the basis of our existence we are selfish, act wishfully, and are controlled by our desires. Our karma has equipped us with consciousness, name-and-form, six sense organs, and feelings. We crave, desire, and cling to this illusory life where birth is painful, disease is painful, death is painful, unsatisfied desires are painful, and union with unpleasant and separation from pleasant are painful.

Buddha himself did not teach reincarnation of a soul. He said:

> "A thought of self (soul) is an error and all existences are as hollow as a plantain tree and as empty as twirling water bubbles. Therefore, there is no self and there is no transmigration of a self. But there are deeds and the continuation of the effects of deeds".

Ego and personal soul are illusions, and the truth can be known only through the experience of enlightenment. Enlightenment is void of any form, but it is a fullness of reality and being.

The ideal of Hinayana Buddhism is Buddha, who stays in Nirvana forever. The ideal of Mahayana Buddhism is a Boddhisattva. He gives up his attainment of Nirvana in order to live in the world like other human beings do so he could help others attain Nirvana and he stays in the universe until all beings realize Nirvana. He takes sins of all beings on himself in order to help them achieve happiness and realization.

Among the basic Buddhist techniques to facilitate enlightenment are six Paramitas. They are charity, ethics, patience, endurance, concentration, and wisdom.

Another important technique is mindfulness: a constant vigilance and awareness of perceptions (objects), body, emotions, and thoughts - and not forgetting oneself in them. Buddha said:

> "Should any person constantly practice these four foundations of mindfulness - awareness of perceptions, body, emotions, and thoughts - just for seven days, one of two results may be expected in him: the highest knowledge of here and now or, if there be yet a remainder of clinging, the state of non-return."

The practice of Mahayana Buddhism can be divided into Sutras and Tantras. Sutras are common teachings and Tantras are secret techniques including discipline, mental equilibrium and quietude, concentration, wisdom, insight into emptiness, creation of visions, dissolution of visions, rituals, consecration of objects, initiations, empowerments, mantras, creation and offering of mandalas, gestures (mudras), postures, ritual music and dance, recitation of tantric scriptures, meditations, etc.

Tibetan Buddhism and Japanese Zen Buddhism are most famous for their practical ways to realization for people active in common, regular life. Compared to Indian yoga, they do not require physical asceticism, departure to homelessness, hermitage, etc. although many have become hermits, monks and nuns in their schools. However, they require a change of view and attitude toward the world and they require meditation exercises.

TIBETAN BUDDHISM

Buddhism and tantric practices came to Tibet from India. According to Annutara Tantra, two basic kinds of yoga existed in Tibet. The first kind was the Nirvanic path described in the book called "Yoga of Great Symbol." The second kind of practice was represented by six yogas of Naropa: yoga of heart, clear light, sleep, illusory body, bardo (after-death-state), and consciousness transference (Phowa). Some add, also, yoga of non-existence of ego. Lately, mainly three yogas are used: Maha, Anu and Ati. The highest technique of Ati yoga is Dzogchhen. Dzogchhen is a meditation without concepts and belongs to the Nirvanic path.

Tibetan schools derive their traditions from Guru Padmasambhava who came to Tibet from India on an invitation of the Tibetan king, Trhison Deucen. Then, Guru Padmasambhava invited an Indian pandit Vimalamitra to Tibet to help him spread Buddhism. Their most famous followers were Longchenpa and King Jigmelingpa. Those two propagated Dzogchhen, which is still preserved today. After the occupation of Tibet by the Chinese army and the escape of the Dalai Lama to India, the Tibetan teachings and meditation techniques came to the West. The most sacred Tibetan texts containing effective meditation techniques, like "Mahamudra" or "Kunzang Lamay Zhellung," were translated into English and other languages. "Kunzang Lamay Zhellung" describes in great detail a number of most effective and most secret tantric meditations - mainly mantras and visualizations - and attitudes that quickly lead to realization. Even Hindus themselves were regarding Tibetan meditation techniques as higher than the Hinduistic ones; and in search for realization they were traveling to Tibetan lamas and monasteries.

Dzogchhen is regarded as the highest meditation technique in Tibetan yoga. Dzogchhen is difficult to describe and usually is transferred from a master to the student by imitation. One description of Dzogchhen rendered by Tilopa is:

> "Do not meditate, do not think, do not imagine, do not reflect. Keep your mind in it's natural state."

Another instruction is to do nothing, just relax, rest in the quietude, and just be. Another one: "Keep your mind unshaped." Still another highly regarded meditation technique, similar to Dzogchhen, is Mahamudra. Mahamudra uses analysis of thinking and mind as well as direct insight into the mind's nature.

A theoretical basis for Tibetan meditations is the teaching called Madhyamika. Madhyamika propagates the middle path of "not this, not that," the path of emptiness and equilibrium which is beyond the extremes of opposites, i.e. beyond concepts. This idealistic philosophy, with adjustment to the western way of thinking and science, is explained in the first part of this book.

ZEN BUDDHISM

Bodhidharma came from Southern India to China in 520 A.D. where he put foundations to the Chan Sect of Buddhism. Buddhism spread to Korea and from Korea to Japan where it was given the name Zen Buddhism. The Rinzai School of Zen (intellectual one) was formally established in Japan in 1191 A.D. and the Soto School of Zen (quietism) in 1233 A.D. Zen puts the emphasis on the immediate, direct intuitive experience (prajna) of Satori (realization) rather than on the doctrine or intellectual knowledge (vijnana).

Virtues of a Zen man are charity, precepts, humility, energy, work, constant meditation, and wisdom. The Zen man is asked to cleanse himself from affective contamination and from intellectual interference in order to realize a life of spontaneity and freedom. He has to perceive the world as it is.

In order to realize, he can be given various techniques. He can be given a mantra; a mondo (a task leading to the comprehension of the impersonal consciousness); a koan (an illogical, unsolvable task); or other forms of meditations, concentrations, or mental exercises.

For example, by maximally forcing his mind to solve an unsolvable task (koan), he comes to an obstacle called "a great doubt block" where he must give up his intellect, thinking, feeling and ego. When he gives up and surrenders, he can experience Satori. Giving up his ego removes the contradiction between ego and universe. Of course, this cannot come without the maximal initial effort.

CHRISTIAN MYSTICISM

Christian mysticism is similar to Bhakti yoga, Guru yoga, and teaching of Bodhicitta. According to historical documents, Christianity originated from a combination of the sect of Essens in Israel and of Indian Buddhism. There are statements about existent records affirming of Christ being in India and learning Buddhism in the Lhadang monastery of North India. From there, he brought Bhakti yoga, teaching of Bodhicitta, and rituals. Buddhism, at that time, was already 500 years old, and yoga was 200 years old. Even if Christ tried to adjust these ideas to the Jewish religion, his teaching of love for all people was in such contradiction to the old testament teaching about Jewish people being superior and chosen to rule the world that he was crucified for his ideas.

A christian mystic loves Christ as his ideal and his god. He believes that Christ suffers his pains with him and enjoys his happiness with him. He repeats prayers to Christ and repeats Christ's name with love, silently and constantly (christian mystic Kerning stated that Christ's real name was Iehoshuah). He surrenders his will and personality to Christ and does only what Christ wants. He wishes nothing for himself and is afraid of nothing. He has unlimited faith in Christ and Christ's teaching. He believes that Christ will do everything for him in the best possible way, and he leaves everything up to Christ. He believes that Christ is taking over his sins and imperfections on himself. He believes that Christ knows all his thoughts, feelings, and motivations. He voids his mind for Christ (vacare deo). Every body, including his body, is Christ's body. Christ is conscious of everything of which he and other people are conscious. Christ is omniscient.

Some christian mystics believe that they have died - drowned at baptism - and that Christ is living instead of them. Not they themselves anymore, but Christ is perceiving, feeling, thinking, and doing everything instead of them. The whole universe is Christ. Only Christ's consciousness exists. They see Christ in everything, feel Christ's presence constantly and love Christ in everything.

To a mystic, Christ is a manifested god. Father god is the unmanifested godhead. Holy Spirit pervades everything. This Trinity is a unity. The goal of a christian mystic is to unify himself with god. When he becomes identical with Christ, he becomes identical also with the other two aspects of god.

At the beginning of Christianity many mystics attained realization; but the installation of dogmas, creation of monasteries, and requirement of celibacy for priests very effectively prevented the next generations from obtaining realization. Thus, to attain realization in christian churches gradually became more difficult and finally it disappeared.

Under the influence of eastern philosophy, Christianity is presently trying again to introduce the experience of realization into it's practice. One example is the trapist monk and writer, Thomas Merton. The German mystic Eckhardt is an example of the most advanced christian mysticism.

Because the majority of mystics rejects reason (intellect) and puts the emphasis just on faith, they cannot work themselves up to the Ultimate Truth and Reality. In all religions, only those who have the courage and intelligence to go beyond dogmas and conventions of their churches are able to realize the truth.

SUFISM

Sufism is Islamic esoterism, that is, muslim mysticism. The basic teaching is the divine unity of being. This can be realized only if the human ego disappears before the Reality in accordance with the fundamental muslim doctrine that there is no other substance aside from the one Reality (there is no god except Allah). When the veil of selfishness is lifted, it unveils the Spirit and - at that time - one can see things the way they are. The Spirit (ar-Rúh) that is above the thought forms and knows the Truth resides in the heart of man. The consciousness of a common man is imprisoned in a state similar to a dream, in a state of forgetfulness.

Sufism offers a twofold path to realization: a philosophical path (mahrifa) and a path of love (mahabda). Only the Absolute is real; all else is an unreal, impermanent illusion. According to Islam, the Absolute was a hidden treasure that wished to manifest itself in order to know itself; therefore, it created the universe.

A spiritual master (sheik) introduces his students to the spiritual path by initiations into meditation. This exoteric path consists of prayers, alms, fasting, and pilgrimage to a holy place. Alcohol and pork are forbidden. Islam characteristically does not recognize casts and classes, and all people are considered to be equal. On the other hand, Islamic requirement to spread their faith by fire and sword is contradictory to the proclaimed way of love.

The inner path recommends the practice of virtues like sincerity, endurance, poverty, remembrance, constant awareness, contemplation and invocation (dhikr). Sufism does not require celibacy. Sufism requires only a temporary abstention from sex and some fasting during a certain period. One has to constantly repeat the name of god (Allah), which is a vehicle to the basic principle, until the believer identifies himself with this name. Repetition of the divine name can be done in an assembly of believers aloud for one or two hours; or it can be done alone - silently or aloud. This can be accompanied by rhythmic movements, dance (of dervishes), music, and drums. During the repetition of the god's name, one can use a rosary (beads) for counting the number of repetitions. A believer first asks for forgiveness of his sins. Then he prays for the blessings from the prophet Mohammed and asks for peace (salaam). Finally, he prays for the realization of the divine unity. This has to be done five times a day. A sufi also has to repeat the god's name constantly during his activities. According to Sufism, god himself is who invokes, is invoked, and is also the invocation.

TANTRIC SEX

Tantric sexual practices are esoteric meditation practices sometimes used in Yoga and Budhism. When having sex with a person we love, we should imagine that he (she) is a divine being and that he (she) has realization, but maybe just does not know that he or she has it. We should concentrate our attention on the feeling of love and on the unity with that person. We forget ourselves, and feel that we are the loved person and identify ourselves with the other person by samayama type of concentration. In this way, sex becomes meditation.

During tantric sex, both man and woman should have the same goal (i.e. realization) and the same behavior. Their aim has to be relaxation, not orgasm. They should avoid ejaculation and orgasm during tantric sex. Therefore, the movements should be slow and relaxed. Whenever the orgasm or ejaculation are imminent, the movements should be stopped. Breathing has to be deep. Behavior has to be gentle, compassionate, and without passion, excitement, or forcefulness.

After three quarters of an hour to three and half hours, a state of indifferent, objective observer and of quietude and silence can appear. At that time, one should stop the movement and continue in the sexual unity without movement. The foreheads should touch each other. Talking is forbidden and is not needed during the entire act because what one person is experiencing, the other one is automatically experiencing. The combination of not thinking, loss of the feeling of personality, and relaxation accompanying sex can induce the experience of realization.

CHEMICAL COMPOUNDS

Diethylamide of Lysergic Acid (LSD), Ketamine, Mescaline, and other chemicals can influence the functioning of the brain in such a way that they enhance attention, concentration, and imagination. They help to remove the feeling of body and personality and support the apperception (primary perception without additional concepts). Thus, these chemicals facilitate the awareness of the immobile basis of consciousness as a contrast to increased amount of imaginations and perceptions.

The chemical compound itself usually does not bring about realization. Successful use of such compounds for attainment of realization usually requires additional factors such as a quiet relaxed environment, classical music, a half-sitting position with closed eyes, and, especially, an experienced instructor who has or had realization and knows how to direct the person using the chemical compound toward realization.

Some drugs are harmful and prevent realization. For example, stimulants (like amphetamines), cocaine, alcohol, the sniffing of glue or gasoline damage the brain permanently and are obstacles to realization.

The relatively safest and most effective of chemical compounds are LSD and Ketamine. LSD, under the above mentioned favorable conditions, leads to realization in about 80% of the cases. Such realization lasts from several hours to several days. LSD is not an addictive drug. Contraindications to LSD are gravidity, manic-depressive illness, history of a psychosis or a disposition to it, unfavorable environment, and/or unsuitable supervision after its use for approximately ten to twelve hours. Unsuitable supervision includes everyone who has not had realization. As soon as realization is attained, no further supervision is needed. Ketamine is also safe and has very few sideeffects, but the racemic Ketamin is less effective.

When the chemical compound is eliminated from the body - many times even sooner - realization disappears. Although realization attained by chemicals is not different from realization attained by meditations, a permanent realization cannot be attained by chemicals. When the feeling of personality returns, and with it wanting or fearing, the realization disappears. Permanent realization can be attained only by knowing the workings of one's own mind through meditations and by unselfish life.

EVOLUTION AND REALIZATION

Survival of an individual requires fear of death and of pain as well as identification with the body and a belief in one's mortality. Beings who were not afraid of death and did not care about their bodies or did not believe in the reality of the world were eliminated by the natural selection process of evolution.

On the other hand, the evolutionary selection of exactly perceiving, adequately feeling, and precisely thinking brains is directing evolution in such a way that there are arising individuals able to understand and feel the reality of the nature of the universe. However, many of those persons mistakenly connect the feeling of reality with objects and not with consciousness.

Some thinkers in old eastern cultures saw facts of evolutionary process but were not able to explain them properly because of the lack of a scientific approach to them. Instead of an evolutionary theory they created a mistaken theory of reincarnation of souls.

In the past, many societies did not tolerate persons who publicly dared to help others attain realization. Even if their intelligence, usefulness, and effectiveness were greater than that of their peers, the worldly and religious rulers tried to get rid of realized persons. The rulers felt they might lose their power over those having realization. Also, realized persons were charismatic, and people listened to them and followed them. Therefore, the rulers tried to remove realized persons from public life, sometimes even having them killed. Because of that, the number of realized persons did not increase significantly. For this reasons, some realized persons organized secret societies so their members could not be easily identified and persecuted.

Other important factors lowering the number of human beings with realization were their indifference to sex and their lack of desire to have children. Many persons who had one or two experiences of realization entered monasteries in hope that they could attain realization there again. Almost all religions considered sex a vice and an obstacle to a pious life. Therefore, they forbade monks and nuns to have children, and they required celibacy. In this way, religions very effectively removed the possibility of increasing the number of persons with realization through heredity.

If during twenty generations (that is for about 500 years), everybody who has or will have realization have children, then according to genetic calculations, everybody will get realization easily. Eventually people will begin to be born with realization, and realization will be happening spontaneously. Because in the past the conditions were just opposite, the movements founded by realized persons degenerated into religions; and the realization disappeared from religions gradually.

Presently, the process of natural selection is influenced by civilization and spreading of democracy. Therefore, persons with realization can survive easily in spite of the feeling of unreality of their personality and the universe. In the free part of the world, these people are not usually persecuted openly by organized religions or by the state. They can publish their experiences. Also, they can help spread realization by having children; which means they can utilize heredity, rearing, and education about realization.

PROGRESS

According to Tantras the universe has no beginning and no end. There was no time when the universe did not exist and there will be no time when it will not continue to exist. The universe is in a constant process of change: evolving, involving, and finally dissolving - expanding and contracting rhythmically. One universal cycle lasts, according to Tantras, for several billion years. In the past, there were infinite numbers of such cycles, and there will be an infinite number of such cycles in the future. During its dissolution, the universe collapses into one point (presently called singularity), and then it disappears into a timeless and spaceless emptiness. From this spaceless emptiness again arises one point from which a new universe is created by explosion of that point. The new universe is always somewhat different from the previous one. Not every universe creates conditions for the evolution of human beings similar to the present ones. According to Tantras, presently about 3,000 planets with human beings similar to us exist in the universe. In addition to human beings, there are many more planets with lower and higher developed beings in this universe.

From the standpoint of eternity, there is no final progress and no final regression or degeneration. But from the present standpoint of transient human beings limited by time and space, a constant evolution and progress or regression and degeneration exists. The universe is not perfect, but is still the best possible one. If it were perfect, it would become absolute, i.e. emptiness and it could not exist. This imperfection of the universe science calls asymetry.

Although science and technique progressed more during the last 50 years than during the previous 1,000 years, people themselves changed very little. They are as selfish, envious, violent, malicious, prone to deceive, and reckless to other people and other beings as they were thousands of years ago when they lived in the animal kingdom without science and civilization. Their personal, racial, and international relationships lag far behind the progress in science, as does their relationship to animals and to the rest of nature. Humankind can perish just because of its too successful, smart brain with very little wisdom. People are reproducing excessively, recklessly ruining the environment that supports them, and producing weapons of mass destruction.

Technological progress and progress in the economy, organization of the society, communications, politics, psychology, religion, medicine, and other fields of science are important; but such progress alone cannot substantially improve life on earth and satisfy people. Moreover, if misused, progress can be used for dictatorship, war, and other selfish causes thus making the life on earth substantially more miserable - full of suffering, pain, and death. Even the most ideal political institution can be misused. Only the understanding and knowledge of the unity of consciousness can substantially improve the life on earth. The most important progress - the one that can make everyone happy and content, and that can remove unnecessary suffering - is the knowledge of our own consciousness and awareness of what we really are.

If a person is selfish, ignorant, and emotionally or mentally disturbed, he or she cannot live in harmony with himself or herself, and others. A collective of such individuals is much less able to live in harmony because the possibility of frictions in a group increases not linearly but exponentially.

If any group separates itself from the rest and selfishly emphasizes only one aspect of life (for example, race, nationality, religion, economy, politics, power, money, pleasure, science, art, philosophy, faith, etc.) at the expense of the other aspects or groups, it finally inevitably fails. Any division of mankind into interest groups brings conflicts, fights for power, wars and misery. This are the reasons why realization cannot be spread by organized groups, religions, nations, races, etc. It can be promoted only individually and in families.

When man wants to live in harmony with the environment, he must first create harmony within himself. Because the basic element of mankind is an individual, the change must begin with an individual and take into consideration his natural inclinations. Such change in an individual must be voluntary, based on his knowledge and convictions, and not dictated from outside by pressure and force.

Trying to change only others and not ourselves improves nothing, and ends up with our accusing others. To blame others for our unhappiness can induce a sick, paranoid state.

To know the truth, to see our improper reactions, and to be willing and able to change our behavior according to the truth will bring a permanent happiness and contentment to the person and, also, to the community of such persons. If at least every tenth person on this earth had realization, life would begin to change into paradise. Even the worst political organization of society could not prevent a paradise on this earth if a majority of people had realization.

Tradition and progress are opposites. While studying traditional methods to realization, we should not be biased and closed to new, unconventional approaches. The most important thing is to know oneself, i.e., realize pure consciousness. Pure consciousness is our origin, life, goal and destiny which none finally can avoid. Also, it is the only way to the Ultimate Truth and to freedom from ignorance, fear, and unnecessary suffering.

MATURATION

Every cell has a mind. When a human ovum and sperm unite, their minds also unite. Fertilization of an ovum begins an evolution of a new human being. This is the most important event in human life. The influence of conception on a human life is the greatest one - greater than delivery, Oedipus complex, inferiority complex, or other known physiological and psychological factors influencing a human life. The closer the environmental influences are to conception, the greater consequences they have on the foetus.

A foetus not only has consciousness, but also perceptions, emotions, and thoughts long before delivery. The foetus thinks by concepts because it does not know words. It also learns to move, swallow, and control its movements.

After conception, the second most important milestone in life is usually the delivery because this is a big and painful change. After delivery an infant learns to perceive new objects and to differentiate them from it's body. The infant finds that there are things independent of his will and discovers the concept of causality. To that which cannot be changed by its will, the infant ascribes a stability and reality. Repeated experiences with objects outside of its body reinforce the feeling of existence of a reality independent of oneself. The infant concludes that something exists, which is common to all perceptions and is always the same. Because the infant does not see the subtle inner changes and life in the objects, he thinks that a dead, dull matter without consciousness and intelligence exists. This is a beginning of the delusion about existence of lifeless matter.

The child learns first to see its ego, person, and body as something different from the consciousness which he feels he is. The child calls himself the same way as others call him. For example, he does not say: "I want it" but "Johnny wants it." Later, he creates a feeling of "I" and learns to differentiate it from thoughts, emotions, and perceptions. Then he identifies himself with the body and isolates it from the rest of the world.

We have been doing samayama type of concentration on our body during our entire lifetime. Therefore, we feel strongly that we are just this body. We create a selfish barrier and a resultant paranoid attitude toward the world. As a result of our self-preservation drive and of the desire for pleasant feelings, we often treat others recklessly. In order not to feel guilty, we create theories and beliefs justifying our reckless and cruel deeds. For example, in order to be able to eat meat, we create a belief that only man has a soul and that animals do not have one; or that animals are just living, not thinking machines without consciousness, awareness, intelligence, etc. In order to satisfy our self-preservation drive many of us believe that we have a personal soul which will be living eternally even after our physical death. Or, some people believe that their religion or nation is predetermined to rule over others and, therefore, they are permitted to take advantage of, cheat, abuse, and even kill others.

Maturation can stop at the level where we feel ourselves to be identical with our bodies and with the ego feelings. We see our bodies and egos as different from other objects, emotions, and thoughts. The next stage of maturation, where we feel ourselves to be at a unity with the universe, does not come. Instead, especially with older persons, maturation can progress to one level further. Many older persons can stop feeling themselves as being a body and identify themselves only with the ego feeling. At this level, they create a theory about a personal soul independent from the body because they wish to survive the physical death.

If maturation continues in the right direction, we learn to see the ego feeling as a transient, impermanent imagination and we develop an impersonal observer of ego and of personality. This way, we return to the original unity of ourselves and the universe, but with the important difference: now we understand ourselves and the universe, know how to differentiate between its individual components and processes, and see its eternal, immobile substance. Thus we do not cling to our personal existences and do not fear death. We let go of that which must die and we remain that which cannot die and is eternal.